*To all the curious people out there.
Keep asking questions!*

### Publisher's Note

This book invites you to explore twelve astonishing worlds of discovery, from Medicine and Sport to Food and Space.

We couldn't include everything, of course, but we've tried to squish in as many important discoveries as possible. (And some daft ones, too: we couldn't possibly leave out the eighteenth-century pooing duck robot.)

It's often impossible to know exactly who discovered things first. Many inventors built on earlier breakthroughs. And lots of bright ideas occurred to people in different places at different times, so some of the examples we've included might not be the absolute earliest. (Archaeologists are always finding earlier examples, too.)

They're all fascinating, though – and by hopping our way around the globe, we've aimed to give a sense of the inspiring spirit of discovery that has driven people everywhere, throughout human history.

A note about dates:
Dates before the year 1 are marked 'BCE' ('before common era').
Dates after the year 1 are only marked 'CE' (common era), if we felt that was needed for clarity.

Here's how to find your way around the twelve worlds of discovery:

**1.** The **introduction** to each chapter gives you a brief overview of the subject – plus a bonus fun fact.

**2.** A spectacular, imaginative **'map'** of each subject whisks you on a tour of key characters and discoveries. You'll find explorers, artists, scientists, sportspeople, ancient breadcrumbs and the Eiffel Tower. You'll also meet unknown ancestors who discovered everything from fire to cheese.

**3.** The **story** pages provide lots more amazing facts about everything from life in space to whale song. You can also learn about important tools of the trade, such as telescopes, nanobots, recipe books and leeches.

First published in the UK in 2023 by Alison Green Books
An imprint of Scholastic
1 London Bridge, London SE1 9BG
Scholastic Ireland, 89E Lagan Road, Dublin Industrial Estate,
Glasnevin, Dublin D11 HP5F
www.scholastic.co.uk
Designed by Zoë Tucker and Ali Halliday
Thank you to Philip Parker for checking our facts.
Thanks also to Stephanie Blankshein, Nadieh Bremer
and Jules Howard for their invaluable help and advice.
The publisher has made every effort to ensure
that all facts are correct at the time of going to press.
Text and illustrations copyright © Thiago de Moraes, 2023
HB ISBN: 978 0 702300 51 6
All rights reserved. Moral rights asserted.
Printed in China
Paper made from wood grown in responsible and
other controlled forest resources.
9 8 7 6 5 4 3 2 1

Thiago de Moraes

# DISCOVERY ATLAS

*Amazing inventors, explorers and artists from all around the globe*

ALISON GREEN BOOKS

*What are those lights shining in the night?
What does that leaf taste like?
What happens if I chip this rock
with another?*

Questions. Lots of them. We humans just can't help being curious about the world we live in. And the more curious we are, the more we discover. That's just as well because, if our ancestors hadn't made so many discoveries, you wouldn't be holding this book. You certainly wouldn't be able to read it, because we wouldn't have invented writing. (Or paper. Or printing.)

We weren't the first kind of human to start discovering things. Long before we evolved, ancient early humans had a knack for creating stuff, too. A million years ago, they'd already worked out how to use fire and chip stone tools.

Modern humans like us have walked the Earth for a mere 300,000 years, but we've come a long way in that time. We've gone from telling stories about the Man in the Moon to sending actual people to walk on the Moon. Along the way we've come up with countless ideas, tools and medicines that make our lives better, safer and more interesting.

Some things were discovered so long ago, it's hard to believe we haven't always had them. Imagine a world without numbers or writing; without farming or furniture or houses or pants. Imagine a world without *chocolate*.

And we haven't just discovered *things*. We've discovered new *ideas*, too, like dividing our days up into hours, or giving ourselves surnames: a surprisingly recent invention. We also came up with the notion of giving children homework. (Who said all ideas were good ideas?)

What drives us to keep on discovering? Curiosity is a huge force: we just love to know how things work. But invention is often a matter of necessity, too. For instance, if a new disease comes along, we need to work hard to find a cure for it.

We also have great imaginations, and our busy brains love to be entertained. We draw pictures, make music, dance and tell stories like no other creature on Earth. These things are just as important to us as all the brilliant discoveries we've made in medicine or maths.

Sometimes it's plain old boredom that makes us try new ways of doing things. Perhaps that's why we invented thousands of different microwave meals and hundreds of types of pasta, so we never have to eat the same thing two days in a row. (Luckily, we also invented sport, so we can work it all off.)

Not all our discoveries are good, sadly. We've created terrible weapons. We've come up with horrible ideas that led us to kill or enslave people. We've damaged our planet in all sorts of ways; but the same brains and inventiveness that led us to do those things can also help us find ways to improve the world and do things better.

When you look around, it feels as if almost everything has already been discovered, right? But that's really not true. In fact, the more we learn, the more we find there is to discover. All over the world, millions of scientists, thinkers, engineers, artists and explorers are using their curiosity to create things we can't even imagine.

Or maybe we can.

You've probably got some great ideas in your head right now. With a bit of hard work, *your* ideas could be the ones that change the world in years to come. Pizza, bicycles, teddy bears, the internet, video games: someone thought of all of those things. (Not the same person. That would be crazy.) So, there's nothing stopping *you* from discovering the next thing that will change the world.

In the following twelve chapters you'll discover some of humanity's most astounding discoveries and the people who made them. We'll go from Neanderthals cooking their dinner to robots landing on Mars, via a very big shark.

Ready to explore?

*Thiago de Moraes*

**Thiago de Moraes**

# A TIMELINE OF DISCOVERY

**TOOLS**
At least 2.6 million years ago
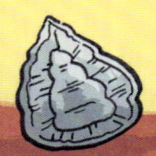

**FIRE**
At least a million years ago

**ART**
At least 45,000 years ago

**MUSICAL INSTRUMENTS**
At least 40,000 years ago
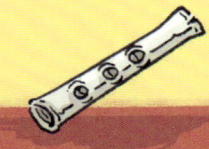

**BREAD**
At least 14,000 years ago

**CHOCOLATE**
1500 BCE
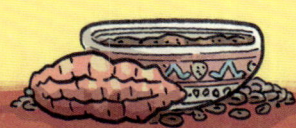

**FOOTBALL**
300 BCE

**ICE CREAM**
200 BCE

**TOILET PAPER**
500 CE

**SPECTACLES**
1280s CE

**ELECTRIC LIGHT**
1879 CE

**MOTOR CAR**
1886 CE

**AEROPLANE**
1903 CE

**ELECTRONIC TV**
1920s–30s CE

**SLICED BREAD**
1928 CE

**It feels as if humans have lived on Earth for ever, but we're actually the new kids on the block. A lot happened before we came along...**

Travel back 13.8 billion years, and our universe started with the Big Bang. Planet Earth formed 4.55 billion years ago. Then it took about another billion years for the first teeny-tiny life forms to appear. A big jump in time brings us to the dinosaurs, some 250 million years ago. Then take another big leap to around six million years ago, when our first ancient human ancestors showed up.

Modern humans like us only evolved around 300,000 years ago, but we've been very busy ever since. Here are a few key things we've invented and discovered during our brief time on Earth.

### FARMING
10,000 BCE

### PET CATS
7500 BCE

### CITIES
4500 BCE

### WRITING
3400 BCE

### MONEY
3000 BCE

### PRINTING PRESS
1450s CE

### VACCINES
1796 CE

### PHOTOGRAPHY
1830s CE

### BICYCLES
1860s-70s CE

### TELEPHONE
1876 CE

### HUMANS IN SPACE
1961 CE

### PERSONAL COMPUTER
1970s CE

### INTERNET
1970s-80s CE

### SMARTPHONE
1992 CE

### YOUTUBE
2005 CE

# The discovery of
# Technology

#### MAKING THINGS BETTER BY MAKING BETTER THINGS

Long before modern humans like us evolved, our ancestors were already creating ways to make life more comfortable, efficient and safe. They started with sharpened rocks. Two million years later, we're making cars that can drive themselves.

In between, creative, curious humans have invented all manner of handy techniques and objects that have changed the way we live. We've learned how to use energy from fire, wind, water and even the Sun. We've created materials that are lighter and harder than anything that exists in nature, and machines that can do maths faster than the fastest human mind.

There have been so many amazing technological discoveries that it's impossible to fit them all into one chapter. There wasn't space to mention radio, microwaves, pianos, nylon, helicopters, drones and many other inventions that we take for granted. (But don't worry, video games are so important, they had to make the cut.)

Of course, not all technology makes things better. Alongside the countless brilliant inventions, we have created others that harm us and our environment: horrible weapons; mountains of waste, polluting chemicals. Luckily, new inventions and clever ideas can sometimes help solve these problems, too.

### FUNNY, THAT . . .
In the 1700s, a French inventor called Jacques de Vaucanson created a mechanical duck that could eat and (more importantly) poo like a real duck. It was very impressive, but for some reason the fashion for pooing duck robots didn't catch on.

## 13 ◆ NIKOLA TESLA
*1856–1943, Croatia/USA*
Tesla believed his inventions were better than those of Thomas Edison, his former boss. He certainly created loads of incredible things, including motors that are still used today, and early X-ray, radio and wireless technology.

## 12 ◆ ELECTRIC LIGHT
*Late 19th century, USA*
Inventor Thomas Edison worked out how to use electricity to generate power and light. Lewis Howard Latimer's many innovations included a filament that made the first light bulbs last much longer. Bright sparks.

## 11 ◆ AEROPLANES
*1903, USA*
The first successful flying machine was created and flown by American brothers Orville and Wilbur Wright. It was basically made from sticks and fabric, so they had to be brave as well as brainy.

## 10 ◆ STEPHANIE KWOLEK
*1923–2014, USA*
A chemist who created brand-new materials like Kevlar®. It's extra-light, stronger than steel, and is used in everything from tennis racquets and spacecraft to bulletproof vests.

## 9 ◆ ELIJAH McCOY
*1844–1929, Canada/USA*
Machines have to be oiled – but how do you oil a moving train? McCoy invented a system that was so good, railway engineers always asked for 'the real McCoy'.

## 8 ◆ COMPUTERS
*Mid-19th century, UK*
These two computer pioneers were way ahead of their time. Charles Babbage designed the Analytical Engine, an early mechanical computer. Ada Lovelace wrote the very first computer program to make it do calculations.

## 14 ◆ MOTOR CARS
*1886, Germany*
Lots of people tried to create a 'horseless carriage' (or 'car' as we'd call it.) German inventor Karl Benz's version changed the world. It was a little three-wheeled vehicle with a small petrol engine. That chap would go a long way.

## 15 ◆ ALAN TURING
*1912–1954, UK*
Turing created the principles behind artificial intelligence – the idea that machines can think for themselves. (He also invented crafty code-breaking devices used in World War II.)

## 16 ◆ ISMAIL AL-JAZARI
*1136–1206, Mesopotamia*
An engineer who created wonderful, programmable machines. His Elephant Clock had mechanical birds and dragons, and a fella who bashed a drum on the elephant's head.

## 17 ◆ ALEXANDER GRAHAM BELL
*1847–1922, UK/North America*
Bell is credited with inventing the telephone (but he didn't want a phone in his study in case it distracted him from his work.)

## 18 ◆ HEDY LAMARR
*1914–2000, Austria/USA*
This famous Hollywood actress was also an inventor. During World War II she invented frequency-hopping technology that could stop torpedoes being detected. Her technology was later used to create Bluetooth, Wi-Fi and GPS.

## 19 ◆ GRACE HOPPER
*1906–1992, USA*
Thanks to Hopper's work, we can now program computers using words instead of symbols. She also found the first computer bug: an actual moth that got stuck inside the computer.

## 20 ◆ PLASTIC
*Mid-19th century, USA*
One of the first plastics was invented by John Wesley Hyatt. Celluloid replaced ivory in everything from billiard balls to piano keys, and elephants were forever grateful.

## 21 ◆ WRITING
Around 5,400 years ago, Mesopotamia
It took humans thousands of years to figure out how to jot things down by scratching marks on clay. Did they write novels? Or poems? Nope. Just records of stuff they'd bought and sold.

# The discovery of Technology

*A dazzling dramatisation, including magnificent machines, clever cogs and awesome automata.*

### ① TOOLS
*At least 2.6 million years ago, Africa*
Way before modern humans evolved, our ancient ancestors were already chipping one rock with another to make rough stone knives. So much easier for cutting a slice of wildebeest.

### ② FIRE
*At least 1 million years ago, Africa*
It was a huge breakthrough when our ancient ancestors worked out how to control fire. Suddenly they could keep warm and safe, work in the dark and, most importantly, have roast dinners.

### ③ WHEELS
*Around 5,500 years ago, Mesopotamia/Europe*
The first wheels weren't used for vehicles, but for making pots. Much later, humans worked out how to build wheeled carts and ploughs and get animals to pull them. A great help for humankind. (Not so much fun for an ox.)

### ④ JAMES BLYTH
*1839–1906, Scotland*
Blyth worked out how to turn wind power into electricity. His turbine didn't impress local villagers, though, who thought electricity was 'the work of the devil'.

### ⑤ STEAM ENGINE
*1st century CE, ancient Egypt*
Greek inventor Heron of Alexandria built the first steam engine to power a mechanical toy. Some 1,700 years later, Scottish inventor James Watt perfected a steam engine that powered whole factories and led to the invention of steam trains. That's progress.

### ⑥ GRANVILLE T. WOODS
*1856–1910, USA*
Woods invented a lot of things, including a way of sending telegraph messages to and from moving trains. This prevented many accidents and saved lots of lives.

### ⑦ ARCHIMEDES
*287–212 BCE, ancient Greece*
A mathematical genius and inventor. He created useful things like pumps and pulleys. He supposedly made some crazy ones, too, like using giant mirrors as a heat ray to burn enemy ships.

### ㉒ TELEVISION
*1927, USA*
The first all-electronic TV was invented by Philo T. Farnsworth when he was just 15 years old. (Sadly, he didn't invent TV programmes, so he had nothing to watch.)

### ㉓ RALPH BAER
*1922–2014, Germany/USA*
Thank Ralph for video games. He had the idea of making a game that could be played on a TV. The Magnavox Odyssey was very basic, with really simple games (but they were very good games.)

### ㉔ KODJO AFATE GNIKOU
*20th/21st century, Togo*
This inventor built a 3D printer entirely out of electronic rubbish from landfill sites. As well as recycling waste, his printer has printed artificial knees for operations.

### ㉕ THE INTERNET & THE WEB
*Late 20th century, USA and UK*
Americans Vinton Cerf and Bob Kahn were the brains behind the internet: a network that links computers together. British computer scientist Tim Berners-Lee invented the World Wide Web, which made it easy to share information across that network. Both inventions changed the way we live (even if we mainly just look at silly videos.)

### ㉖ SIMON THE SMARTPHONE
*1992, USA*
The world's first smartphone. Made by IBM, Simon was big and clunky, but had email, note pad, calculator, sketch pad and more. It could even make phone calls!

### ㉗ PARO THE ROBOT SEAL
*2004, Japan*
Cuddly Paro is actually a super-sophisticated robot that reacts when you stroke it. Its inventor, Takanori Shibata, created it to help comfort elderly people with dementia.

### ㉘ EMOJIS
*Late 20th century, Japan*
These fun little symbols were created as a way to save space in messages. Thanks to this important invention you can now send a smiley face – or a smiley poo – to a friend.

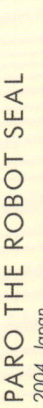
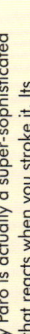

# Dying to make it work
## YOU'VE GOT TO FALL BEFORE YOU CAN FLY

Some inventors are so keen to test their creations that they skimp on health and safety a bit. Or a lot. These guys all came to a sticky end whilst putting their inventions into practice.

### OTTO LILIENTHAL
*1848-1896, Germany*

Lilienthal was a brilliant engineer who was fascinated by the idea of flying. He studied how birds flew, then designed and built wonderful gliders: aircraft without engines, which soared on the wind. He made over 2,000 successful flights . . . until, sadly, his luck ran out. One fateful day, his glider nosedived and crashed, and he ended up splatted on the ground.

### FRANZ REICHELT
*1878-1912, Austria/France*

Reichelt wanted to create a parachute that would save pilots if they fell from a plane. He tested lots of designs using dummies, then he experimented with a human: himself. He strapped on his parachute, jumped from the top of the Eiffel Tower in Paris and . . . yup, ended up splatted on the ground.

### JEAN-FRANÇOIS PILÂTRE DE ROZIER
*1754-1785, France*

De Rozier was determined to be the first person to fly a hot-air balloon. His first brief flight was a success, so he designed an even better balloon and set off to fly across the English Channel. Tragically, the balloon caught fire and crashed, and de Rozier and his companion ended up (you guessed it) splatted on the ground.

# Amazing everyday inventions
## YOU MEAN WE HAVEN'T ALWAYS HAD THESE?

### BRIGHT BUTTONS

Buttons were a great invention: people have decorated their clothes with them for thousands of years. Button*holes* were an even better invention. Before some clever clogs came up with them in the thirteenth century, we used all sorts of uncomfortable and fiddly things to keep clothes on our bodies, from belts and laces to brooches and pins.

### RUNNING HIGH ON BATTERY

The first battery, invented by Alessandro Volta in 1800, was a big, wobbly pile of metal discs. These days, neat little batteries power everything from toys to computers – and the technology keeps getting better. Now inventors are working on shoes that would generate and store energy as you walk, so you could charge your phone with them.

### THE WRITE STUFF

What do you write with? Pencil? Felt pen? Lucky you. Ancient Egyptian scribes used pens made from reeds. Ancient Romans scratched letters into small wax tablets. In ancient China, the tools of writing – brush, ink, inkstone and paper – were so prized they were called 'The Four Treasures of the Study'. It must have taken ages to write a shopping list.

### NOW YOU SEE IT, THEN YOU DIDN'T

Bad luck if you needed glasses in the past. Although ancient Greeks and Romans tried using curved bits of glass to magnify things, it wasn't until the 1200s that some Italian monks decided to prop two tiny lenses in a frame and perch them on top of their noses – a proper sight for sore eyes.

# Magnificent Inventors

## EVERY TRICK IN THE BOOK
*The Banu Musa: 9th century, Baghdad*

There were once three brilliant brothers whose dad was a highwayman. That sounds like the start of a fairy tale, but it's actually true. The boys were the Banu Musa (it means 'sons of Musa') and they were astonishing scientists and inventors.

In a surprising career move, their dad gave up plundering to become a talented astronomer. He was soon best pals with the Caliph, the grand ruler in Baghdad. The Caliph noticed that Musa's sons were very bright. He sent them to study at his House of Wisdom: a huge place of learning where scholars came from miles around to use its fabulous library and discuss ideas and inventions.

The boys wowed everyone with their scientific discoveries and inventions. Their most famous book, *The Book of Ingenious Devices*, describes a hundred extraordinary machines, from mechanical fountains to a robot that plays the flute. The machines were so startling, many people thought they were magic.

## MAN OF MANY, MANY TALENTS
*Leonardo da Vinci: 1452-1519, Italy*

Leonardo is best known for creating the *Mona Lisa*: the world's most famous painting of a lady sitting looking at you. But he did much more than that.

Engineering, physics, astronomy, map-making, mathematics, the human body: Leonardo thought about it all. His notebooks, which run to more than 7,000 pages, are filled with so many plans for new contraptions, you might think a whole army of inventors drew them, not just one beardy man. Most of his ideas were far too advanced to be built in his lifetime, but that didn't stop him devising flying machines, mechanical robots, calculators, diving suits, submarines, parachutes and even a way of generating solar power. He wrote most of his notes backwards, too, so you'll need a mirror if you want to read them.

## DRIVING MRS BENZ
*Karl and Bertha Benz: 1880s, Germany*

Karl Benz had a problem. He'd invented the first modern motor car, but no one wanted to ride in it. Strangely, the idea of rocketing along in a rickety, three-wheeled basket, powered by a huge noisy engine, didn't appeal to most people.

Enter Mrs Benz: Karl's wife, Bertha. Bertha had helped fund the development of her husband's car. Now she decided to give it some publicity. Without telling him, she popped her two kids in the car, and drove 90 km to visit her mum.

The journey wasn't exactly smooth. Bertha had to refuel using stain remover from a pharmacy. She had to fix the car with a hat pin and her garter. She even invented brake pads, by getting a shoemaker to strap some leather round the worn-out brakes. But when Bertha's extraordinary journey was reported in the papers, suddenly everyone wanted to drive their own car.

## SAVING LIVES AND HAIRDOS
*Garrett Morgan: 1877-1963, USA*

Garrett Morgan learned how to fix machines at an early age. He opened a repair shop, and soon started inventing amazing solutions to all sorts of problems.

Morgan's first major invention was the smoke hood: an early gas mask to protect firefighters. It helped save countless lives — as did his next invention: a traffic signal. People were just starting to drive cars around cities, and there were accidents left, right and centre. Morgan's traffic signal had three positions: stop, go and wait, making the roads much safer for drivers and pedestrians alike.

To top it all, Morgan created a very successful range of hair care products. He even accidentally invented a hair-straightening cream. He tried it out on himself and on the neighbour's dog. It worked so well that his neighbour didn't recognise the poor mutt. No one knows what the dog thought, but he probably preferred the natural look.

TECHNOLOGY 15

# Tools of the Trade
## GREAT INVENTIONS THAT CHANGED HISTORY

### CLOCKS

Today, everything from your oven to your car can tell you the time, but imagine how tricky it was keeping time before reliable clocks were invented. The first mechanical clock was created in China in the eighth century by an astronomer called Yi Xing. It banged a drum every 15 minutes, which is useful but probably a bit annoying after a while.

### PRINTING PRESS

Before printing, every single book had to be copied by hand. They'd invented various ways to print books in China, but it was still a slow process. Things really speeded up in the 1450s, when German goldsmith Johannes Gutenberg converted a wine press into a printing press. With cheap, mass-produced books, information and knowledge could spread all round the world.

### COMPUTERS

We'd tried for centuries to build 'calculating machines', but the first true computers weren't built till the 1940s. They weighed tonnes and took up whole rooms. Luckily, computers have got smaller, and a *lot* more powerful since then. A modern smartphone has 100,000 times more processing power than the computer that helped put people on the Moon in 1969.

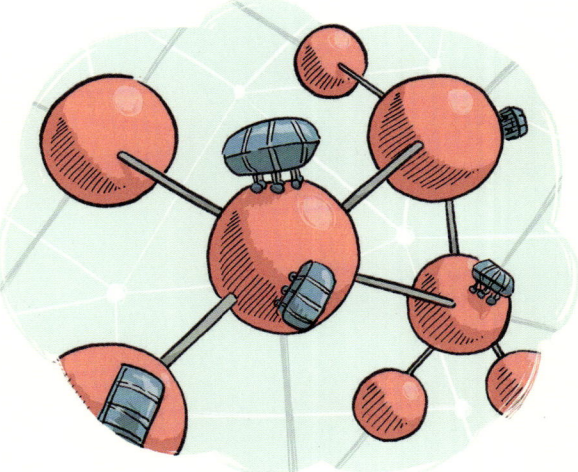

### NANOBOTS

One of the most exciting new technologies is so small you won't be able to see it. Nanobots are the tiniest robots imaginable: a million of them could fit on the head of a pin. Scientists are trying to build these mini-machines to help with everything from fighting cancer to cleaning up pollution.

# The discovery of
# Food

## WE ARE WHAT WE EAT

Food is the fuel we need to grow and live. But it's also much more than that. Food is right at the heart of every culture in the world. From earliest times, eating a meal together has been one of the best ways to make friends and show that we care about one another.

But what we eat has changed hugely over time. For millennia, early humans simply ate whatever they could find and hunt. (Once they'd worked out how to make fire, they could cook it, too.) It was only a few thousand years ago that we started to plant foods such as wheat, barley and rice. We learned how to keep animals, too, like goats, sheep and chickens. We settled down — and got creative, whipping up ever more fancy dishes to please ourselves and impress our friends.

Gradually, as we explored the world, we discovered each other's delicacies. All sorts of familiar foods, such as potatoes, tomatoes, rice and spices, only used to grow in certain parts of the world. It's only in the past few centuries that everyone's discovered them.

Today we can grow meat in a laboratory and have a takeaway delivered by drone. The way we make our food has changed beyond imagining — but we still enjoy eating together.

### FUNNY, THAT . . .
For ancient Romans, no meal was complete without a dollop of *garum* — the empire's favourite sauce. Made from fish guts and blood, it was left to ferment for months in the sun, until it was good and smelly. It's apparently incredibly tasty. Fancy a dollop on your chips?

**1 TEA**
*Around 4,700 years ago, China*
It's said that mythical Chinese Emperor Shennong discovered tea when some leaves blew into his pot of hot water. Many years later, poet and tea-lover Lu Yu wrote *The Classic of Tea*, a book that teaches how to grow, brew and drink it.

**2 CHOCOLATE**
*Around 3,500 years ago, Central America*
Chocolate was originally consumed as a bitter drink flavoured with spices. Later, the Aztecs and Mayans thought it had magical powers. Chocolate made its way to Europe in the 1500s but didn't become a sweet, delicious bar till 1847.

**3 BOILING**
*From prehistoric times, Europe/Asia*
We've been cooking food in hot water for a long time. One theory even proposes that our Neanderthal cousins could have boiled their dinner using leather bags.

**4 CLARENCE BIRDSEYE**
*1886–1956, USA*
Birdseye saw how Inuit fishermen preserved fish by freezing it in the Arctic air. It inspired him to invent his own way of freezing food. He tried it on meat, veg and even an alligator, but he's best known for his fish fingers.

**5 RICE**
*Around 7,000 years ago, China*
Rice is incredibly important – half the world's people depend on it. Japanese mythology even has a god called Inari who protects the rice crop.

**6 FARMING**
*Around 12,000 years ago, western Asia*
Humans used to move around with the seasons, to find plants and animals to eat. As we worked out how to plant seeds and tame animals, we could stay in one place and farm the land.

**7 FLEMMIE KITTRELL**
*1904–1980, USA*
A nutritionist who realised that many poor people around the world have 'hidden hunger': they feel full, but aren't eating the right foods to keep them healthy.

**8 COOKING**
*From prehistoric times, Africa*
Did our ancient ancestors drop the first chunk of meat into a fire by accident or design? We'll never know, but it must have tasted great, as we've never stopped cooking since.

**9 PASTA**
*13th century, Italy*
From African couscous to Asian noodles, people eat boiled dough all over the world. Italians began eating pasta in the Middle Ages, when it was a food for the rich, often served with sugar. Pasta now comes in over 300 different shapes.

**10 ALEXIS SOYER**
*1810–1858, France*
When Ireland was hit by a terrible famine, this famous chef saved lives by setting up soup kitchens. He also cooked a slap-up Christmas feast for over 20,000 poor Londoners.

**11 KEBABS**
*From ancient times, Europe/western Asia*
Who doesn't love a kebab? It's said that, in the Middle Ages, Turkish soldiers skewered chunks of meat on their swords and cooked them over a fire.

**12 INSECTS**
*Throughout human history, worldwide*
People eat all sorts of insects: termites, crickets, ants and other creepy-crawlies like deep-fried tarantulas. As we try to eat less meat, they could become useful food for the future.

**13 CHEESE**
*Around 10,000 years ago, Europe*
Farmers may have invented cheese by accident, by storing milk in animal stomachs, where it curdled. A 3,200-year-old hunk of cheese was found in the tomb of ancient Egyptian scribe, Ptahmes. Sadly, both man and cheese were way past their best.

**14 ANTOINE-AUGUSTIN PARMENTIER**
*1737–1813, France*
When potatoes first arrived in Europe, many were too scared to eat them. This pharmacist campaigned to prove that they were safe and delicious. He even hosted spud-based banquets. Thanks for all the chips!

**15 WEDDING CAKES**
*17th century, England*
Ancient Romans crumbled a plain cake over a bride's head for good luck. In England in the 1600s, cakes with white-sugar icing showed how rich you were. Now huge, extravagant wedding cakes are popular all over the world.

**16 SOYA**
*At least 5,000 years ago, China*
We can use soya beans to make everything from oil and soy sauce to tofu and a type of milk. No wonder Chinese Emperor Shennong declared soya to be a sacred plant.

**17 DABBAWALAS**
*From the 1890s, India*
Possibly the world's oldest food-delivery system. Dabbawalas have been carrying takeaway lunches to busy office workers for over 125 years. They deliver 80 million home-made hot meals every year, on foot or by bike, all without apps or computers.

**18 COFFEE**
*9th century?, Ethiopia*
Legend says that coffee beans were discovered by a goatherd who noticed his goats got all excitable after eating berries from a local bush. We now drink two billion cups of coffee every day.

**19 PEPPER**
*Around 4,000 years ago, India*
Pepper was so rare and expensive, it used to be worth its weight in gold. It was even stuffed into the mummified nostrils of Egyptian pharaoh Ramses the Great. You'd think it would make him sneeze.

### 20 SALT
*From ancient times, worldwide*
Salt is a very ancient seasoning. It was used to preserve food, and was so important, wars were fought over it. Some wages were even paid in salt.

### 21 LIVE BLACKBIRD PIE
*16th century, Europe*
To impress guests at banquets, rich hosts served pies with live birds in them. The poor birds were put in after the pie was cooked, and flew out (possibly covered in gravy) when it was cut.

### 22 WHEAT
*Around 11,000 years ago, Mesopotamia*
Wheat was one of the first wild grasses that humans learned to cultivate. Just as well, or we'd have no bread, cakes or biscuits to eat.

### 23 ROBOT RESTAURANTS
*21st century, worldwide*
In some modern restaurants, robots cook the food, serve it, and even wash up the pans. Best watch out for flywheels in your soup.

### 24 SUSHI
*19th century, Japan*
Sushi's ancient history started in China, but the raw-fish-and-sticky-rice sushi we eat today developed in Japan. Sushi chefs train for years, but few know how to prepare pufferfish sushi, which is deadly if you don't get the poison out.

### 25 FERRAN ADRIÀ
*1962– , Spain*
This ingenious chef used science and art to make food look and taste extraordinary. His famous dishes include tomato sorbet, caramelised eggs and edible smoke foam.

### 26 ASTRONAUT FOOD
*20th century, Russia/USA*
Space food must be super-light, and keep well without a fridge. You also don't want crumbs floating about in zero gravity. Early astronauts had mushy pastes in tubes. These days they can have meals created by expert chefs

### The discovery of
# Food
A delicious depiction, featuring cake mountains, fields of pasta and rivers of tea.

# You say 'potato'... I say, 'What's that?'
## HOW FOOD TRAVELLED THE WORLD

For thousands of years, people ate very different foods, depending on what grew well on the continent where they lived.

Then in 1492, European explorers sailed across the Atlantic Ocean and bumped into the Americas (which they hadn't known existed). Although they didn't turn out to be the friendliest dinner guests, one of the happier results of their journey was that everyone around the world started to discover each other's foods.

For people everywhere, dinner would never be the same. Some foods travelled from east to west, and from north to south. Others went the other way around. Crucially, we can now find chips and bananas wherever we go.

### FROM THE AMERICAS

POTATOES PUMPKINS
MAIZE PEPPERS
TOMATOES
CHOCOLATE
TURKEYS

### FROM EUROPE, AFRICA AND ASIA

PIGS CABBAGES
ORANGES BANANAS
LEMONS
GRAPES OLIVES
COWS

# Delicious mistakes
## FAVOURITE FOODS INVENTED BY ACCIDENT

### GETTING TO THE CRUNCH

In the 1890s, American physician John Kellogg was trying to create a super-healthy food for his patients. He accidentally left some wheat dough out overnight, but decided to roll and bake it anyway. It made rather tasty flakes. He tried it again with corn – and created corn flakes. They proved incredibly popular (especially once his brother added some not-quite-so-healthy sugar to them.)

### A CRISP CUSTOMER

We don't really know who invented crisps, but there's a fun legend about it. In 1853, African American chef George Crum became frustrated when a customer kept complaining that his chips were cut too thick. Crum finally chopped them into super-thin, crispy slices. Oddly, the customer loved them (and later so did we all.)

### SELLING LIKE COLD CAKES

On a hot day at the 1904 World's Fair in St Louis, USA, ice-cream seller Arnold Fornachou sold so many ice creams that he ran out of cups. Did he pack up and go home? No, he bought waffles from a nearby stall, rolled them up, and created some of the world's first ice-cream cones. Pretty cool.

### FORGOTTEN TO PERFECTION

In the 1830s, British pharmacists John Lea and William Perrins cooked up a recipe for a sauce that one of their customers had eaten in India. They didn't like the taste, though, so stuck it in the cellar. Two years later they tried it again: the fermented sauce now tasted delicious! They named it Worcestershire Sauce, after their home town.

# Tools of the Trade
## THE BEST IDEAS SINCE BEFORE SLICED BREAD

### RECIPE BOOKS

If you've cooked something tasty, it makes sense to jot down the recipe. The world's oldest surviving cookbook was carved into clay tablets nearly 4,000 years ago in Babylonia (modern-day Iraq). The recipes are surprisingly similar to food that is still eaten in that region today, such as lamb stew with onions, garlic and leeks.

### TAKEAWAYS

Fast food seems very modern, but it's been around a long time. Two thousand years ago, ancient Romans could drop by a *thermopolium* (it means 'a shop that sells hot things'.) These were nifty little snack bars set into walls in the street, where they could get some wine, meat, fish, cheese and nuts to eat on the go.

### FRIDGES

Before fridges, the best way to keep your food cool was to pack it in ice – not easy in a hot country like Australia. So it's no surprise that inventor James Harrison created one of the first commercial ice-making machines there in 1854. It was great for factories, but way too big for your kitchen. It took another 60 years for small home fridges to finally come along.

### CUTLERY

Eating with your hands is very, er . . . handy, but we still invented all sorts of cutlery. People in China started using chopsticks some 5,000 years ago. For centuries, Europeans used knives and spoons (and their fingers), but forks didn't catch on everywhere till the 1600s. Although they existed much earlier, the first people to use forks were considered vain, and even quite shocking.

# The discovery of
# Planet Earth

## GLOBE-TROTTING AND ISLAND-HOPPING

For as long as humans have existed, we've had the urge to go exploring. From Africa, where the story of our species began, groups of our ancient ancestors travelled to almost every part of the planet. Mostly on foot. No wonder it took them tens of thousands of years. Humans eventually settled in almost every part of the globe, from dry deserts and frozen icefields to fertile plains and forbidding forests.

But we still didn't understand our planet very well. It took us ages (and lots of bonkers theories) to work out that the Earth is a sphere. It took us even longer to discover the exact shapes and sizes of the continents, or the distances between places, because the tools we needed to measure such things were only invented quite recently.

In each new place we came to, we discovered new animals, new plants and even new weather. By studying them we came to understand how all living things on Earth depend on each other to survive.

We're still exploring today, peering into massive cave systems, sending robots under ice sheets, and stumbling across unknown plants and creatures in remote forests. There's still so much to find out about this huge wet rock we all live on.

**FUNNY, THAT . . .**
Volcanoes smell like farts. They emit sulphur: a substance used to make matches (amongst other things), which happens to be incredibly stinky. It's also quite dangerous and can cause serious injury if you inhale a lot of it. Not unlike some parps.

## 1 FIRST STEPS
*Around 1.8 million years ago, Africa*
Early humans evolved in Africa, then gradually settled all over the world. Homo erectus set off first. Homo sapiens (that's us!) followed over 1.5 million years later. (On foot, which took ages – at least they didn't have to queue at the airport.)

## 2 ERATOSTHENES
*Around 276-194 BCE, ancient Greece*
This clever clogs was the first to work out the circumference of the Earth. He measured the angle of the Sun, and saw how it cast different shadows in different places. Then he did some nifty maths, and got it almost spot on.

## 3 MUHAMMAD AL-IDRISI
*1100-1165, Morocco*
A famous map maker. He sent travellers all over the known world to gather information, so he could create an amazing book of maps for the king of Sicily. His maps have south at the top, unlike most modern maps which have north at the top.

## 4 LONGITUDE
*18th century, England*
For centuries, many ships were wrecked because they didn't know how far east or west they'd sailed. Then amateur clockmaker John Harrison made a clock which sailors could use to work out how far they'd travelled from their starting point. Problem solved!

## 5 ARTHUR TANSLEY
*1871-1955, UK*
A pioneering botanist who realised that everything on Earth exists in an ecosystem: an environment where all the plants, animals, bacteria, climate and soil have an effect on one another.

## 6 THE POLES
*20th century, Arctic/Antarctica*
In 1909, American explorers Matthew Henson and Robert Peary announced that they'd finally reached the North Pole. It had taken several dangerous attempts over many years. Two years later, Norwegian explorer Roald Amundsen and his chums were first to the South Pole.

## 7 GETTING TO THE AMERICAS
*At least 15,000 years ago, Siberia/Alaska*
Humans only arrived in the Americas quite recently. It's thought some people walked over from Siberia to Alaska. The land they walked on disappeared under the sea when the last Ice Age ended.

## 8 STEPHEN BISHOP
*1821?-1857, USA*
Mammoth Cave in Kentucky is the longest-known cave system in the world. Several kilometres of its terrifying, pitch-dark depths were mapped by Bishop, an enslaved African American who became an expert tour guide.

## 9 MASSIVE MUSHROOM
*2,000-8,000 years old?, USA*
The largest living thing on our planet isn't the blue whale. It's a fungus, discovered in Oregon in the 1990s. It covers nearly 10 square kilometres – bigger than a small town.

## 10 DIRECTIONS
*From prehistoric times, worldwide*
From earliest times, people calculated directions based on how the Sun moves across the sky. The ancient Aztecs grouped everything – regions, gods, dates and even colours – according to north, south, east or west.

## 11 THE HOT TUB OF DESPAIR
*Discovered 2015, Gulf of Mexico*
Weirdly, you can get lakes at the bottom of the sea. Brine pools contain super-salty water, which is more dense than the ocean above. They generally kill any poor creature that falls into them. Luckily, explorers used a remote-controlled vessel to find this one.

## 12 ALEXANDER VON HUMBOLDT
*1769-1859, Germany*
Von Humboldt travelled the world studying plants, animals and environments, and came to the groundbreaking conclusion that everything in the universe was interconnected. (He also nearly electrocuted himself with electric eels.)

## 13 TRISTAN DA CUNHA
*Discovered 1506, South Atlantic Ocean*
This tiny island has the most remote human settlement on Earth. People only started living here in 1810. Today there are around 240 residents (and just nine surnames).

# The discovery of Planet Earth

An intrepid exploration of the globe, including deep caves, towering mountains and a really big mushroom.

**21 WAYFINDING**
*Around 3,000 years ago, Polynesia*
Long before modern navigation tools were invented, sailors from New Guinea crossed the vast Pacific Ocean, guided only by their knowledge of stars, birds and ocean currents. They settled on hundreds of islands from Fiji to Hawaii.

**23 ANTARCTICA**
*Discovered 19th century, Southern Ocean*
The ancient Greeks imagined that there must be a frozen continent at the south of the planet, but it wasn't till 1820 that Russian sailor Captain von Bellingshausen finally spotted it.

**24 NEW ZEALAND**
*Discovered 13th century, Oceania*
The last major land mass on Earth to be settled by humans. Polynesian sailors finally discovered it a few hundred years ago. It was worth the wait – it's really lovely.

**14 EUNICE FOOTE**
*1819–1888, USA*
An amateur scientist who discovered that, when the Sun heats carbon dioxide in our atmosphere, it causes climate change. Sadly, her work was ignored by other scientists for decades.

**15 SOLO ROUND-THE-WORLD FLIGHT**
*1933, USA*
The first person to fly solo around the world was Wiley Post. It took him just under eight days (with quite a few stops) to make it from New York to, er . . . New York.

**16 INGE LEHMANN**
*1888–1993, Denmark*
What's inside our planet? No one was quite sure until Lehmann discovered that Earth has an inner core that is a huge, solid ball of white-hot iron.

**17 GLADYS WEST**
*1930– , USA*
A brilliant mathematician, West led the team that programmed a computer to create a precise model of the Earth. Her work formed the basis of the GPS system, which is now used all over the world to help us navigate.

**18 TOP OF MOUNT EVEREST**
*20th century, Himalayas*
The highest spot on Earth, nearly 9 km above sea level. First to reach it were explorers Tenzing Norgay and Edmund Hillary in 1953. It was freezing cold, incredibly dangerous, and hard to breathe in the thin air. Lovely views, though.

**19 SEISMOSCOPE**
*2nd century, China*
One of the first tools to measure earthquakes was created by Chinese scholar Zhang Heng. It was a jar with eight dragon heads around the top. When a quake happened, the dragon nearest the direction of the tremor dropped a ball from its mouth, into the mouth of a toad below.

**20 KATIA KRAFFT**
*1942–1991, France*
Krafft studied volcanoes really closely. She and her husband Maurice stood on active volcanoes all over the world, filming and studying eruptions – until a blast tragically killed them both.

**22 TIM FLANNERY**
*1956– , Australia*
There are still many new animal species to be discovered. Flannery has found over 30, including a couple of tree kangaroos (cute, furry creatures that look quite different from non-tree-based kangaroos.)

# Drifting apart
## THE DISCOVERY OF PANGAEA

If humans had lived 299 million years ago, we might have found it a lot easier to travel around. That's because all of the continents we have today were stuck together in one huge *super*continent called Pangaea.

Scientists have been figuring this out for over a hundred years, working out how the land masses fitted together – like a giant jigsaw puzzle. To us, Pangaea looks like a big jumble, with modern-day North America butting up against North Africa, and India squashed between the other end of Africa and Antarctica.

Gradually, over millions of years, Pangaea split apart, creating the continents we have now. Geologists have since discovered that several other supercontinents had formed and broken apart during the 4.5 billion years that the Earth has been around. And our continents are still on the move today – very, very slowly drifting together again.

# Maps, maps, maps

## FINDING OUR PLACE IN THE WORLD

For most of human history we had no way of making accurate maps. Long-distance journeys were a complicated, risky business that often involved navigating by the Sun, stars or ocean currents. Here are some early maps we made as we tried to find our way around.

### BABYLONIAN MAP OF THE WORLD

The earliest surviving world map is a carved clay tablet over 2,500 years old. It's not for finding your way around. It's more about local mythology, and describes the world as Babylonians understood it. The city of Babylon sits at the centre, surrounded by other local cities and an enormous sea.

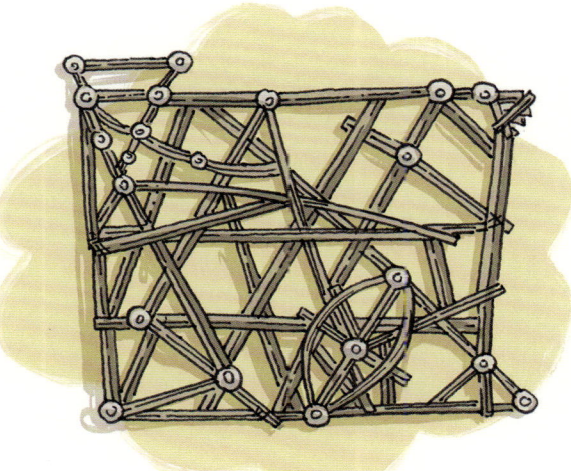

### PACIFIC ISLANDS SAILING CHART

Seafarers in the Marshall Islands created extraordinary charts called *rebbelib*, to help them navigate the vast Pacific Ocean. The charts, made from sticks and shells, reminded them of the position of islands (the shells) and the currents and swells in the ocean (the sticks).

### HERE BE MONSTERS

Map makers in medieval Europe imagined that all sorts of crazy creatures lived in the sea. They filled their maps with sea serpents, dragons, ichthyocentaurs (a mixture of human, horse and fish) and even a fearsome sea-pig, who oinked fear into the hearts of sailors.

### MERCATOR PROJECTION

How do you make a flat map of a round world? In 1569, Flemish map maker Gerardus Mercator had a good go at it. His map was very popular, but it had a big problem. To make it work, he distorted the size of the continents, so northern countries look a lot larger than they actually are.

# Tools of the Trade
## STEPS IN THE RIGHT DIRECTION

### POLAR FOOD

In 1911, two teams raced to be the first to reach the South Pole. British explorer Robert Falcon Scott led one team. Norwegian explorer Roald Amundsen led the other. A problem for both teams was what to eat: there's not much choice (and no supermarkets) in the Antarctic. The explorers consumed the odd penguin. (Scott's team liked theirs stewed in redcurrant jelly.) They also ate a lot of seal. Amundsen undercooked his seal meat, and ate his penguins raw. It sounds grim (and not something you want to try), but it preserved the vitamin C in the meat, and helped keep him healthy. It wasn't the only reason he won the race to the Pole, but it certainly helped.

### POLYNESIAN BOATS

Early Polynesians built extraordinary boats that allowed them to travel across the Pacific Ocean, where they discovered and settled on a huge number of islands. The boats were up to 20 metres long, and could carry a couple of dozen people, plus food for the journey, and even their livestock.

### SEXTANT

This clever instrument, invented in the 1700s, helped sailors work out where they were at sea. It measured the angle between the horizon and the Sun, Moon or stars. Sailors could then use these angles to calculate their position. Better than waiting to ask a passer-by.

# The discovery of
# Medicine

## YOU MIGHT WANT TO PUT SOME POO ON THAT

Got a headache? No problem. We'll just drill a hole in your skull using a sharp stone and let some air out. That might sound bonkers today, but for thousands of years it would have been considered a perfectly sensible way to treat someone. (Still, please don't try it at home.)

Keeping healthy has always been a battle. Throughout history, we've been trying to figure out how our bodies work, and how to treat wounds and diseases. Some ancient theories were genuinely daft, but other treatments were surprisingly effective – like the discovery that the bark of the willow tree could be used to numb pain.

Ancient surgery was often successful, too. But certain things that seem obvious to us today, like washing our hands to get rid of germs, were only discovered a couple of hundred years ago.

The more we learn and the more solutions we invent, the healthier we get and the longer we live. Medical knowledge today is astonishing, but we still don't know everything. Whether it's vaccines against new diseases, or printing skin grafts on a 3D printer, new treatments and technologies are being invented all the time.

### FUNNY, THAT . . .
Medicine was very advanced in ancient Egypt, but doctors still prescribed a few duds or, to be more precise, *dungs*. Animal poo was considered a universal cure back then, and droppings from dogs, donkeys and even gazelle were used to treat all manner of diseases. Yuck.

**1  SUSHRUTA**
6th century BCE, India
A genius surgeon who even pioneered plastic surgery. If someone's nose was cut off as a punishment, he used skin from their face to build them a brand-new schnozz.

**2  LINDA BUCK**
1947– , USA
Buck and her research partner Richard Axel won a Nobel Prize for figuring out how our noses can identify thousands of different smells (sadly including stinky socks).

**3  DILIP MAHALANABIS**
1934–2022, India
Diarrhoea can be a killer. Dr Mahalanabis pioneered a super-simple solution. Literally. It was a drink of salts, glucose and water that stopped patients dying from dehydration.

**4  DANIEL HALE WILLIAMS**
1856–1931, USA
Hale was one of the very first to perform open-heart surgery. He cut open the chest of a man who'd been stabbed, and operated on his heart – a feat of incredible skill. Amazingly, the patient lived another 20 years.

**5  WILLIAM HARVEY**
1578–1657, England
Harvey discovered how the heart pumps blood round the body. He was also doctor to English King Charles I (but couldn't help when the king's head was chopped off in a revolution.)

**6  IMHOTEP**
Around 4,700 years ago, ancient Egypt
The earliest known doctor. When he died, the Egyptians made him a god and prayed to him when they got sick. He'd probably rather they'd seen a doctor.

**7  DNA**
20th century, UK
DNA is the building block of all living organisms. Four scientists – Francis Crick, James Watson, Maurice Wilkins and Rosalind Franklin – worked out the structure of it. Thanks to them, scientists and doctors keep finding new ways to make us healthier.

**23  SIGMUND FREUD**
1856–1939, Austria/Czech Republic
Freud was fascinated by the human mind. He invented psychoanalysis, a way of treating mental health problems by encouraging patients to talk about whatever popped into their heads.

**22  IBN AL-HAYTHAM**
965–1040, Iraq/Egypt
An influential scientist and mathematician. He figured out that it was light rays entering our eyes which makes us see things.

**21  ALEXANDER FLEMING**
1881–1955, UK
Fleming returned from holiday to find that some mould had killed the nasty bacteria he'd been studying. He'd accidentally discovered penicillin, the first antibiotic.

**20  EDWARD JENNER**
1749–1823, England
Dairymaids said they couldn't catch smallpox, because they got a mild disease called cowpox instead. Jenner took pus from a cowpox pustule (yuck) and 'vaccinated' people with it. (The word comes from *vacca*, the Latin word for 'cow'.) Jenner didn't actually use a needle, but many modern vaccines do, and they protect us from lots of nasty diseases.

**19  LADY MARY WORTLEY MONTAGU**
1689–1762, England
This celebrated writer nearly died from a vicious disease called smallpox. Later, in Turkey, she saw a treatment called variolation, which helped protect people from smallpox. She tried to convince English people to do it, too, but many were too scared.

## ⑧ BARBER SURGEONS
*Medieval Europe*
Doctors diagnosed illnesses, but if you needed an operation you went to the barber. Barber surgeons set broken bones, chopped off damaged limbs, bled people using leeches (and gave you a snazzy short back and sides.)

## ⑨ JANE COOKE WRIGHT
*1919–2013, USA*
Wright's work has saved millions of lives. She researched a poorly understood treatment called chemotherapy, and turned it into one of the most important ways to fight cancer.

## ⑩ JOSEPH LISTER
*1827–1912, UK*
Lister worked out that germs caused infections which could kill people. He had the radical idea that surgeons should wash their hands and sterilise their instruments before operating.

## ⑪ ASCLEPIUS
*Worshipped from 500 BCE, ancient Greece*
The ancient Greek god of healing. He carried a staff with a snake coiled round it – still a symbol of medicine today. His worshippers sometimes slept in rooms full of snakes to get better.

## ⑫ HIPPOCRATES
*5th century BCE, ancient Greece*
This physician is famous for creating the Hippocratic Oath, a pledge in which doctors swear not to harm their patients. (Good idea.)

## ⑬ OLA BROWN
*1980s– , UK/Nigeria*
One of the UK's youngest ever doctors, Brown set up Nigeria's first air ambulance service after a family tragedy. As well as treating patients, she learnt to pilot helicopters (probably not at the same time.)

## ⑭ ZHANG ZHONGJING
*Around 150–219, China*
Zhang observed his patients carefully, tested his treatments and recorded the results – all very unusual at the time. His work is still used in traditional Chinese medicine.

## ⑮ FLORENCE NIGHTINGALE
*1820–1910, UK*
During the Crimean War, many soldiers died in dirty hospitals. Nurse Florence brought hygiene, care and organisation, and saved many lives. Afterwards, she set up one of the world's first professional nursing schools.

## ⑯ MARIE CURIE
*1867–1934, Poland/France*
An astoundingly gifted chemist and physicist. Marie, with her husband Pierre, discovered radium – a radioactive chemical which she realised could be used to treat cancer. She also created portable X-ray machines which saved lives in World War I.

## ⑰ ORGAN TRANSPLANTS
*20th century, USA*
In 1954, Richard Herrick got an amazing present from his twin brother, Ronald: one of Ronald's kidneys. It was the first-ever successful organ transplant, and saved Richard's life. Surgeons can now transplant livers, lungs, hearts and even faces.

## ⑱ FINGERPRINTS
*19th century, UK*
Dr Henry Faulds was studying an ancient clay pot when he spotted a mark – and realised it was the fingerprint of the potter. He discovered that each person's fingerprints are unique. Bad news for burglars. Great news for TV cop shows.

## The discovery of Medicine

An extraordinary examination, featuring skilful surgeons, astounding scientists and some very useful mould.

# It seemed a good idea at the time

## ANCIENT REMEDIES AND CRAZY CURES

### A HOLE IN THE HEAD

One of the earliest forms of surgery was trepanation: drilling holes in a person's skull. We're not sure why people did it. Perhaps as a treatment for illnesses? Or as part of a religious ritual? Oddly, turning someone's head into Swiss cheese isn't so popular any more.

### KISS OF DEATH

If drilling a hole in your head sounds bad, how about sleeping with a skull? That's what some healers in ancient Mesopotamia recommended as a cure for grinding your teeth. To make it extra-effective, you had to snog the skull during the night.

### DON'T RUB IT IN

In the 1600s, English doctors had a bizarre 'cure' for sword wounds. They made a paste out of worms, pigs' brains and a sprinkling of grated corpse. Did they rub it on the wound? Of course not. They rubbed the horrid mixture *on the sword that had caused the wound*. Strangely, it didn't work.

### SLOWLY DOES IT

Several medicine books from medieval Europe recommended placing live snails on burns. Amazingly, it may have worked! Scientists today are studying snail slime to see if it can be used in medicine. Not bad for a little creature that takes three hours to cross a road.

### ANOTHER DROP?

Ancient Romans believed they had a sure-fire cure for epilepsy (a condition which causes people to have seizures.) They drank the blood of a gladiator who had been killed in a fight. When gladiatorial fights were forbidden, they drank the blood of executed criminals instead.

# That's a relief
## BRILLIANT DISCOVERIES THAT HAVE MADE OUR WORLD HEALTHIER

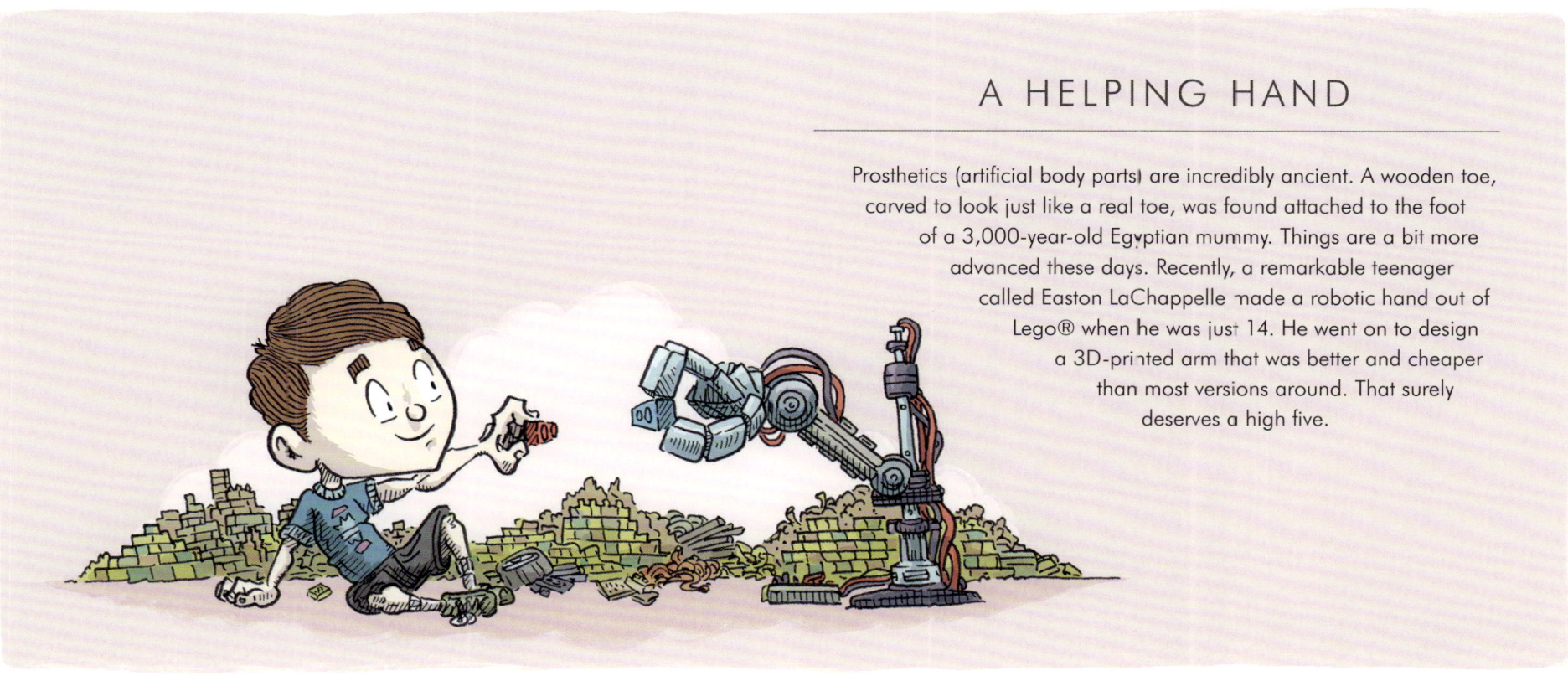

### A HELPING HAND

Prosthetics (artificial body parts) are incredibly ancient. A wooden toe, carved to look just like a real toe, was found attached to the foot of a 3,000-year-old Egyptian mummy. Things are a bit more advanced these days. Recently, a remarkable teenager called Easton LaChappelle made a robotic hand out of Lego® when he was just 14. He went on to design a 3D-printed arm that was better and cheaper than most versions around. That surely deserves a high five.

### SMILE!

Having all your gnashers taken out as a birthday present sounds like a terrible idea (it is). However, that's what a lot of people did before the invention of modern toothpaste and brushes. Cleaning your teeth isn't a new invention, though. For thousands of years, people cleaned their teeth with a chewed-up twig. It wasn't till 1,200 years ago that people in China started making toothbrushes out of hog's hair. Ancient toothpaste contained everything from ground-up shells and ox hooves to charcoal and pumice.

### YOU WON'T FEEL A THING

Imagine having a wound stitched up or a leg chopped off without proper painkillers. Ouch. For centuries, many surgeons just got their patient drunk, then tied them down. Finally, in the 1800s, American dentist William Morton tried using a gas called ether to knock people unconscious. A few years later, Britain's Queen Victoria used an anaesthetic when giving birth to her last two children. Soon everyone saw the sense in being knocked senseless.

# I wonder what's in here?

## A SHORT HISTORY OF DISSECTION

To understand how the body works, you really need to look inside it. That's why early physicians carried out dissection. From ancient Greece to India, they looked inside dead bodies to try and understand how they worked. But cutting open a dead body isn't the cheeriest thing to do, and over time many laws and religions forbade it. In lots of countries, dissection pretty much stopped for hundreds of years.

Attitudes finally started to change in the Middle Ages. People became fascinated by anatomy, and dissection theatres opened up across Europe. Audiences flocked to watch as doctors and surgeons pulled some poor corpse to bits.

There was just one problem: finding bodies to dissect. Scientists mostly used the corpses of executed criminals, but it wasn't enough. Grave-robbing became common. Then two men called William Burke and William Hare took things to extremes in the 1820s, by making some extra corpses to sell. They murdered 16 people before they were found out. Burke was hanged and his body was, er . . . dissected.

Dissection may be gory but, once doctors managed to get a good look inside us, they made lots of discoveries that have helped us look after our health better than ever.

# The nurse will see you now
## HOW AN AWFUL WAR CHANGED OUR HEALTH FOR THE BETTER

In the 1850s, Britain fought a terrible war against Russia in Crimea. Many soldiers died in battle – but many more died from diseases and infections. Appalled by the situation, two remarkable women set off to help.

When British nurse Florence Nightingale arrived at the front, she was horrified by what she found. Soldiers were dying like flies in filthy army hospitals full of rats, lice and fleas. There weren't enough towels, soap, bandages or even food.

Nightingale was organised, super-efficient and obsessed with hygiene. She set her nurses to work, cleaning hospital wards and kitchens. She ordered food and supplies. She even helped wounded soldiers write letters home. They called her 'the Lady with the Lamp', because every night she walked around the wards, checking on her patients. After the war, she campaigned tirelessly for better sanitation, to make sure that never again would so many soldiers die from disease.

Mary Seacole's war was very different, but just as astonishing. Born in Jamaica, Seacole was a resourceful, adventurous woman who loved caring for others. She made her own way to the war zone, and set up a business called the British Hotel: a restaurant for officers and a canteen for ordinary soldiers. Then she began helping out however she could.

She gave refreshments to injured soldiers waiting for hospital ships. She offered traditional remedies to those with less severe ailments. She even ventured on to the battlefield after the fighting, to tend the wounded and comfort the dying. She became a famous and much-loved figure, and soldiers called her 'Mother Seacole', in recognition of her care and kindness.

# Tools of the Trade
## JUST WHAT THE DOCTOR ORDERED

### LEECHES

For centuries, many doctors believed that the best way to cure a disease was to stick leeches on you. The idea was that these bloodsucking slimy worms would literally suck the 'bad blood' out of you. We now know that that doesn't work, but leeches are still occasionally used in medicine to help relieve swelling after surgery.

### PLAGUE MASKS

Bubonic plague was a terrifying disease. It killed millions, and nobody knew how it spread. In the 1600s, European plague doctors thought 'poisonous air' might be to blame, so they wore these creepy masks. They stuffed the long beak with herbs, thinking the nice smell would protect them. It didn't, of course. (And it must have really freaked out their patients.)

### ANTIBIOTICS

In 1877, French scientist Louis Pasteur noticed an amazing thing: that some 'good' bacteria could kill 'bad' bacteria (ones that give you nasty diseases). It was a step on the long road to creating the antibiotic medicines we use today. Before they were invented, millions of people died every year from common diseases and infected cuts and wounds. Keep up the good work, tiny bugs!

### MRI SCANNERS

It's always been tricky for doctors to see what's happening inside your body. Cutting you open isn't a great option, and even the tiniest cameras can't reach everywhere. Then in the 1970s these ingenious scanners were invented, which use a technique called Magnetic Resonance Imaging. Now doctors can see inside you without actually looking inside you. Brilliant!

# The discovery of
# Sport

GETTING THE BALL ROLLING

Who doesn't like a game? Many animals enjoy playing, and humans are no exception. In ancient times, playing games provided great training for all sorts of important skills, such as hunting and fighting, running away from danger and making quick decisions.

But sports also help bring people together as a community. Early sports often took place at religious rituals, such as funerals, festivals and harvests. We still enjoy that feeling of celebration and togetherness today. You only have to look at football supporters chanting on the terraces, or families and friends gathering to watch big sporting events on television.

Most of the games we play today have very ancient origins, but they've changed quite a lot down the years. For instance, modern motor racing isn't so very different from ancient Greek and Roman chariot racing (apart from the lack of horses). Some of the latest esports have games that involve running, jumping, throwing spears or swinging swords. Our ancestors were doing all those things thousands of years ago – but we can now do them from the comfort of our sofa.

**FUNNY, THAT . . .**
Almost anything can be turned into a sport, but some things clearly *shouldn't*. Playing polo with cars was briefly popular at the beginning of the twentieth century. But trying to hit a small ball with a mallet whilst standing on top of a rickety, unstable car was as dangerous as it sounds. Sadly, no one plays it any more.

## 1. HIGHLAND GAMES
*11th century, Scotland*
These traditional Scottish games were a way for warriors to prove who was hardest. Many events still involve throwing very heavy things, including the caber (a huge wooden log); stones and even bags of straw.

## 2. CUJU (FOOTBALL)
*Around 2,300 years ago, China*
This ancient Chinese game is similar to modern football (the name means 'kick ball'). It was hugely popular, with male and female professional teams. Even emperors played it.

## 3. SHAOLIN KUNG FU
*6th century, China*
Fighting doesn't sound very priest-like, but it was Buddhist monks who developed this martial art, so they could protect their monastery from attack.

## 4. DAMBE
*Around 10th century, West Africa*
People have fought each other for sport since ancient times. Dambe is a style of boxing practised by the Hausa people. It started when butchers travelled around selling their wares, and fighting the locals as they went (which is both very friendly *and* very unfriendly.)

## 5. CHARIOT RACING
*7th century BCE, ancient Greece*
Ancient Greeks loved this sport, with its high-speed crashes and moody horses. Spartan princess Kyniska bred the winning team of horses in 396 BCE – the first-ever woman to win at the Olympics.

## 6. SURFING
*12th century, Polynesia?*
We don't know who first rode the waves on a board, but surfing was a huge deal for ancient Polynesians. Some even made the best surfer their chief. Makes sense, given how much time they spent sailing and fishing.

## 7. LACROSSE
*12th century, eastern North America*
A stick-and-ball game first played by Native North American peoples. Unlike today, their rough, tough games had hundreds of players, took place over vast areas, and could last for days.

## 8. PARA SPORTS
*Early 20th century, Europe*
People with all sorts of abilities can take part in sport. Recent advances in technology have helped create a whole new set of exciting sports, including wheelchair basketball and blade running.

## 9. BASKETBALL
*19th century, USA*
PE teacher James Naismith needed an indoor game to entertain his students in bad weather. He nailed two old peach baskets to a wall and got the kids to throw a football into them. His new sport was a slam dunk.

## 10. ICE HOCKEY
*19th century, Canada*
Humans just love hitting a ball with a stick. Ice hockey developed in the British Isles (Queen Victoria's husband Albert played it), but the modern game began in Canada, where ice isn't in short supply.

## 11. SUMO WRESTLING
*7th century, Japan*
The sport of grabbing someone and chucking them around goes back thousands of years. Sumo wrestling started as a religious dance, where wrestlers played the parts of gods, fighting to decide who would rule the land.

## 12. CRICKET
*17th century, England*
Cricket started as a medieval children's game, and went on to become England's national summer sport. It's now played from India to the Caribbean, and is famous for its long games (Test matches take five days) and civilised tea breaks.

## 13. CAPOEIRA
*16th century, Brazil*
Enslaved Africans in Brazil weren't allowed to practise martial arts, so they disguised their fighting as dancing, slowing the moves down and performing them to music. Party for your right to fight.

# The modern Olympics
## BRINGING BACK THE FLAME

The Olympic Games were the biggest sporting event in ancient Greece. People came from far and wide to compete and watch – until spoilsport Roman emperor Theodosius banned them in 393 CE.

Then, in the late 1800s, a French chap called Baron Pierre de Coubertin became obsessed with bringing the Olympics back. Many people thought this was bonkers, but de Coubertin persisted, and the first modern Olympics were held in Greece in 1896. They've taken place nearly every four years since, all over the world.

Some sports, like racing, jumping and gymnastics, were similar to the original ancient Greek ones. Others would seem incredible to Olympic fans today (and to ancient Greeks, too.) Here are some of the more unusual ones, which featured in the early games between 1896 and 1916. They sound really good fun – unless you happen to be a pigeon, of course.

### TUG OF WAR
*Try and drag the other team along till they cross a marker.*

### STANDING HIGH JUMP
*No run-up. Just start with your feet together and jump as high as you can.*

### EXTREME SPORTS
All sports are challenging, but some people really take things to extremes. In fact, we've been risking our necks in the name of sport since time immemorial. For instance, here's a bloke from ancient Crete doing acrobatics on the back of a bull. Please don't be tempted to try that (or any of these other crazy sports) at home.

### DEATH VALLEY MARATHON
A standard marathon race is 42 km – but that's still not long enough for some people. The world's toughest foot race takes place in Death Valley, USA. It's a gruelling 217 km, non-stop, over three mountain ranges, in mid-summer temperatures of over 50°C. Some athletes' shoes have even melted in the heat. Fancy trying it? The record to beat is 21 hours and 33 minutes.

### LIVE PIGEON SHOOTING
*Nearly 300 birds were shot. Ugh.*

### FIREFIGHTING
*Both professional and amateur categories.*

### SWIMMING OBSTACLE RACE
*Swimming under and over things in a river.*

### RUNNING DEER SHOOTING
*Not with live deer, luckily.*

### PISTOL DUELLING
*Shooting at a mannequin dressed in a frock coat.*

### VOLCANO SURFING
Surfing in the ocean is dangerous enough, but it clearly wasn't sufficiently exciting for the people who invented *volcano* surfing. Hurtling down the side of a huge, burning mountain, whilst hoping you won't be hit by scalding lava. That's the life.

### CHEESE ROLLING
You might think that chasing a 4 kg wheel of cheese down a ridiculously steep hill doesn't qualify as an extreme sport. You'd be wrong. Many people are injured in this traditional English contest and have to be carted off to hospital. Spectators have been injured, too, by the speeding cheese, so one year a foam replica was used (but the winner still got an actual cheese.)

# Tools of the Trade
## THE WINNER TAKES THE CLOCK

In sport, we always say that what matters is taking part and trying your best. That's true, but athletes also *really* care about winning – and winning often comes with a prize. In ancient Greece, it was just a simple wreath of laurel leaves. These days it's usually a trophy and a pot of cash. But there are some more unusual prizes . . .

### THAT'S BANANAS

Cycling does seem to like offering odd prizes. One cycling event in Turkey awarded the winner lots (and lots) of bananas. It makes sense: they're a local fruit, and riders like eating bananas during races to give them energy. Let's just hope the winner didn't have to cycle home carrying the whole lot. Even stranger cycling prizes have included a big cheese, a giant sausage, a cobblestone and an actual piglet.

### SNAPPY DRESSERS

The top prize at two of sport's biggest events includes an item of clothing. The leader of the Tour de France (the world's most prestigious cycle race) gets to wear a very bright yellow jersey. Everyone wants to win it now but, when the first rider wore it in 1919, spectators said he looked like a canary.

The winner of the US Golf Masters is awarded a green jacket – but they can only show off in it for a year. After that, they have to send it back to the golf club and are only allowed to wear it there.

### VROOM, VROOM, TICK-TOCK

The winner of the Martinsville Speedway motor race in the USA gets to take home a huge grandfather clock. It's a lovely thing, but what if you won several years in a row? Storage would be tricky – and imagine the racket they'd make every hour.

# The discovery of
# Art

FROM PAINT POTS TO PIXEL DOTS

A great big bronze sculpture? That's art. That eight-legged cat you doodled on the corner of your notebook? That's art, too!

Art is as old as humanity. Archaeologists have found traces of incredibly ancient art all over the globe, even some created by Neanderthals.

Every single society in the world makes art. We use it to tell stories; to express our feelings or opinions, or just to make beautiful things that we enjoy looking at. We might not *need* art in the same way that we need food or shelter, but it's clearly a hugely important part of who we are.

The way we make art has changed down the years, but not as much as you might think. Early humans scratched patterns on shells, painted pictures on cave walls, and tattooed designs on their bodies. We still do those things, but we've also created new tools and techniques which allow us to make art in different ways, from huge modern installations to mobile phone stickers. Our world is packed full of art – too much to fit in one chapter. But turn the page and you can feast on some of the best bits.

**FUNNY, THAT . . .**
Artists can use all sorts of different materials, from ordinary paint and stone, to odd things like sugar, flies or melted cheese. Some contemporary artists have even used lumps of chewing gum or blobs of dried elephant poo on their paintings.

**1. CAVE PAINTING**
*At least 45,000 years ago, worldwide*
From handprints to hunting scenes, our ancestors painted on cave walls all over the world. Did their prehistoric parents tell them off?

**2. CALLIGRAPHY**
*Around 3,000 years ago, worldwide*
How's your handwriting? Calligraphy is the art of writing beautifully. In Japan, calligraphy is even used as a form of meditation.

**3. SCULPTURE**
*Around 40,000 years ago, worldwide*
Tens of thousands of years ago, someone sat down and carved this *Lion Man* out of a mammoth tusk. It's one of the earliest sculptures we know of.

**4. NEANDERTHAL ART**
*At least 65,000 years ago, Europe*
It seems modern humans weren't the only ones to make art. Some scientists believe that ancient cave drawings found in Spain were created by our Neanderthal cousins.

**5. JEWELLERY**
*From prehistoric times, worldwide*
We started making jewellery out of shells at least 100,000 years ago. Once we discovered how to work metal, we could make some serious bling. Even ancient warriors wore hefty gold neck rings to show off their wealth.

**6. MASKS**
*Around 9,000 years ago, worldwide*
People have worn masks for ages, in rituals or just for fun. The Dogon people of west Africa make especially elaborate masks, which they still use in ceremonies today.

**7. MINIATURE PORTRAITS**
*16th century, Europe*
These tiny paintings could be popped in your pocket or hung on a necklace – very handy before the invention of photographs. In the 1500s, English artist Nicholas Hilliard became one of the best wee-picture painters. He used a weasel's tooth to paint the tiniest details.

**8. MARBLE STATUES**
*6th century BCE, ancient Greece*
The ancient Greeks carved incredibly realistic sculptures out of marble. They painted them in bright colours, but the paint's worn off down the years, so now they just look white.

**9. PRINT MAKING**
*7th century, China*
Printing pictures using a carved wooden stamp started in China, but in the 1800s Japanese artists like Hokusai made it really famous. His *Great Wave* has jazzed up everything from banknotes to lunchboxes.

**10. EMBROIDERY**
*At least 3,500 years ago, worldwide*
The ancient art of sewing patterns on to fabric. The 900-year-old Bayeux Tapestry is actually a massive embroidery, almost 70 metres long. Must have taken ages to stitch.

**11. THE RENAISSANCE**
*14th–17th century, Europe*
The Renaissance was a time of incredible creativity and scientific discovery. Artists like Raphael and Michelangelo dazzled the world by painting scenes and people in a more lifelike way than ever before.

**12. POTTERY**
*At least 20,000 years ago, worldwide*
We've made objects out of clay for millennia. The ancient Greeks liked to make beautiful pots decorated with their favourite myths and legends.

### 13. TOTEM POLES
*For centuries, American Pacific Northwest*
These tall, intricate sculptures are carved from tree trunks. They often tell a story, or have a spiritual meaning, and can feature animal spirits like bears, beavers, eagles and whales.

### 14. SELF-PORTRAITS
*For centuries, worldwide*
Who first painted a picture of themselves? We'll never know, but there are all sorts of ways of doing it. In the 1800s, Dutch artist Vincent van Gogh shocked people by painting himself with bold colours and wild brush strokes.

### 15. PHOTOGRAPHY
*19th century, France*
When photography was invented, some artists worried that it would put them out of a job. It didn't, of course. In fact, photography became an art form in its own right.

### 16. FRESCO PAINTING
*Around 4,000 years ago, all round the Mediterranean*
Painting pictures all over your walls was a hugely popular way of decorating a room. The tomb of Nebamun, an ancient Egyptian scribe, is covered in beautiful fresco paintings. Luckily, it was built before he died, so he got to admire them.

### 17. MONUMENTAL SCULPTURE
*From prehistoric times, worldwide*
We've been making enormous sculptures from wood and stone for thousands of years. The huge Moai on Easter Island were carved just a few hundred years ago. We still don't know how the islanders managed to move them.

### 18. INCA TEXTILES
*15th–16th century, South America*
The Incas wove amazing, intricate fabrics. Their textiles were so valuable, people even used them to pay their taxes.

### 19. TATTOOS
*At least 5,000 years ago, worldwide*
Drawing on your body is a very old art form. It's thought ancient Egyptian women were tattooed to protect them during pregnancy, while Māori people of New Zealand have face tattoos that tell all sorts of information about them.

### 20. ILLUSTRATED BOOKS
*From around 500 CE, worldwide*
Before printing, books were written and illustrated by hand. Only the wealthy could afford them – like the Mughal emperor Akbar, who commissioned the *Akbarnama*, the story of his life. Akbar couldn't read, but he could look at the stunningly detailed pictures.

### 21. BRONZE SCULPTURE
*From around 4,000 years ago, worldwide*
Bronze was originally used to make weapons, but artists quickly realised that it made brilliant sculptures – like this spectacular one from the Kingdom of Benin. They melted bronze or brass and poured it into a mould.

### 22. GRAVE GOODS
*From prehistoric times, worldwide*
We've been burying precious objects alongside the dead for millennia – but the grave of China's first emperor takes the biscuit. He was buried with some 8,000 life-sized terracotta statues – an army that's guarded him for over 2,000 years.

### 23. GRAFFITI ART
*20th century, USA*
We've drawn on walls since the Stone Age, but modern graffiti art began in the 1970s, when American artists started decorating everything from underground trains to office blocks.

### 24. TEMPORARY ART
*20th century, UK*
Not all art is made to last. British artist Andy Goldsworthy creates sculptures using things he finds in nature – leaves, stones and even ice. Then he lets them decay naturally.

## The discovery of Art
An enthralling exhibition, featuring prehistoric paintings, staggering sculptures and magnificent masks.

# So . . . what is art?

## IDEAS TO MAKE YOU THINK

We all know what art is, don't we? Well, yes . . . and no. Ever since the late nineteenth century, artists have started to think about art in very different ways. Some have even challenged the very idea of what art is.

## MIND IF I GIFTWRAP THAT?

Husband-and-wife team Christo and Jeanne-Claude turned famous landmarks into huge sculptures by wrapping them in fabric. They wrapped buildings, small islands, a chunk of Australian coastline and even the Pont Neuf Bridge in Paris. That last one took over 40,000 square metres of fabric, 13 kilometres of rope and some 300 helpers. It stood for just two weeks in 1985, before the fabric was taken down and the artwork was no more.

## A HAIRY EXPERIENCE

In 1974, German artist Joseph Beuys had himself wrapped up in felt, then taken by ambulance to an art gallery in New York, where he was locked inside for several days with a real, live coyote. He hoped this piece of performance art would help bring American society together. No one knows how the coyote felt about it all.

## ANYONE NEED THE LOO?

French artist Marcel Duchamp claimed that anything could be art if an artist said it was – even an everyday object you could buy in a shop. His most iconic piece is a urinal. He bought it from a bathroom shop, signed it using a pseudonym and entered it for an art show in 1917. Lots of people thought it was a wee bit silly.

46  Art

## INFINITE NUMBERS OF PUMPKINS

Japanese artist Yayoi Kusama has two favourite themes: polka dots and pumpkins. She's also famous for her Infinity Mirror Rooms, where lights and objects are reflected endlessly around you. In 2016, she combined these ideas in a dazzling roomful of yellow, spotty pumpkins. Visitors stepped inside the room – and became part of the artwork. Mirrors reflected more and more *and more* pumpkins at them, surrounding them with an infinite number of these cheerful, comforting vegetables.

## IS THAT A PICKLED SHARK?

In 1991, British artist Damien Hirst placed a dead shark in a tank of formaldehyde and displayed it in a gallery in London. The idea was to make people think about death (and about sharks, presumably). Lots of people argued about whether or not it was art, but everyone agreed that the piece had some bite.

## MONEY FOR NOTHING

In 1958, French artist Yves Klein painted a room in an art gallery white, and placed nothing in it but an empty cabinet. He called this empty room *The Void*, and held a grand opening to which 3,000 people turned up. In another brilliant move, Klein sold 'zones of empty space' in return for pure gold. All the buyer got was a receipt, which Klein invited them to burn. What does this say about art? No idea. But some people clearly have a lot of spare cash on their hands.

# Tools of the Trade
## GETTING IT DOWN TO A FINE ART

### PAINT

Want to paint? You'll need some colours. The first paints were natural colours like red earth, yellow clay and white chalk. Later we learned to make colours from all sorts of things: red from a mineral called cinnabar; purple from the slime of sea snails, and blue, which was super-expensive, from an incredibly rare stone called lapis lazuli.

### WAX

Surprisingly, a lot of metal sculptures start with wax. Here's how it works. Make your model out of beeswax, then cover it in clay. Bake it till the clay is hard – the wax will melt and drain away, leaving an empty clay mould. Pour hot molten metal inside the mould and leave it to cool. Then crack open the clay and – ta-dah! You have a beautiful metal sculpture.

### PINHOLE CAMERA

Weirdly, cameras were invented long before photography. In the fifth century BCE, Chinese philosopher Mo Ti described how to project an image into a box by passing light rays through a tiny hole. Over 2,000 years later, we finally worked out how to print these images to create photographs (which literally means 'drawing with light'.)

### NFTs

Art used to be something you could touch: marble, metal, paint or wood. Not any more. An NFT, or 'non-fungible token', is a digital work that only one person can own – even if lots of people can see it online. It could be a picture, a video, or even a tweet, and they can sell for huge sums of money (or, more likely, for peanuts . . . )

48

# The discovery of
# Space

## FROM STAR GAZING TO MOON LANDINGS

We now understand that the universe is a vast place filled with planets, stars and all manner of wonderful things. But without our modern technologies, ancient cultures had to find other ways of explaining the sky above them. Ancient Egyptians thought it was held up by a god called Shu. Some tribes in central Asia believed it was the roof of a giant tent.

Gradually we started to understand the cosmos, and Earth's place in it. It took humans a long time to accept that Earth *wasn't* the centre of the universe: that it was just a tiny rock, spinning around an average-sized star, similar to billions of other rocks and stars out there. (It's fine – we're still pretty special, in our own way.)

We eventually progressed from watching planets at a distance to travelling beyond our atmosphere into space. We've set foot on the Moon, and have sent probes to explore other planets. These probes have landed on Mars; sent photos from Pluto, and visited asteroids millions of kilometres away.

Perhaps in future we'll travel away from our tiny planet and try and live on others. We might even find some new neighbours out there.

### FUNNY, THAT . . .
When we first started exploring space, we discovered a little problem: there's no air, which is why astronauts have to wear spacesuits. Without one, your body would blow up to twice its size, the saliva in your mouth would boil and after a few seconds you'd run out of air. And eventually freeze. No suit? Best stay at home.

### 3 CELESTIAL SPHERES
*6th century BCE, ancient Greece*
Ancient Greek astronomers believed that the Sun, Moon, stars and planets rolled around Earth on giant, invisible spheres. They were wrong, but it's a fun idea.

### 6 MAYAN ASTRONOMY
*4th–10th century, Central America*
The Maya created incredibly accurate calendars by studying the stars. They also believed that stars revealed the will of the gods.

### 9 JULES VERNE
*1828–1905, France*
This popular science fiction writer wrote a book where explorers were fired up to the Moon from a massive cannon. Explosive stuff!

### 1 NEWGRANGE
*Around 5,200 years ago, Ireland*
Many cultures built incredible structures which lined up with the movement of the Sun. On the shortest day of the year, the Sun shines directly down the entrance of this massive ancient temple.

### 4 ABD AL-RAHMAN AL-SUFI
*903–986, Iran*
Al-Sufi was the first astronomer to observe stars beyond our galaxy. The Azophi crater on the Moon is named after him.

### 7 POLYNESIAN NAVIGATION
*From around 3,300 years ago, Oceania*
Using their exceptional knowledge of the stars, ancient Polynesians could sail across vast oceans without maps or compasses. Talk about following your star.

### 10 ARTHUR WALKER
*1936–2001, USA*
It's not safe to look at the Sun, so Walker devised solar telescopes which could be launched into space. They captured astonishing images of the Sun's burning corona.

### 2 TELESCOPES
*1608, Netherlands*
Thank you to Dutch spectacle-maker Hans Lippershey for inventing the first telescope. It led to amazing discoveries, as scientists could now see the skies in much more detail.

### 5 GALILEO GALILEI
*1564–1642, Italy*
This brilliant scientist and astronomer worked hard to prove that the Sun was at the centre of our solar system (as Copernicus had thought). The Catholic Church was not amused and sentenced Galileo to be locked up for life.

### 8 HUMANS IN SPACE
*1960s, Soviet Union*
The first humans to travel into space had to be really brave. Soviet cosmonaut Yuri Gagarin was first in 1961. Two years later, Valentina Tereshkova became the first woman in space.

### 11 NICOLAUS COPERNICUS
*1473–1543, Poland*
Using only his eyes and a lot of maths, Copernicus developed a radical new theory: that all the planets in our solar system orbit around the Sun, not around the Earth, as most people then thought.

### 12 PHILAE SPACE PROBE
*2014, European Space Agency*
This sophisticated little robot was the first to land on the surface of a comet. It showed that comets are mostly made of dust, rock and ice – like a giant, dusty slushy.

## The discovery of Space

A cosmic investigation, including grumpy gods, swirling galaxies and a whole lot of junk.

### 13 ALIENS
*20th/21st century, the universe*
Is there intelligent life on other planets? We don't know, but scientists scan the skies for messages just in case. Sadly, no one's got in touch – yet.

### 14 ROMAN ASTRONOMY
*From 8th century BCE, ancient Rome*
Our nearest planets, Mercury, Venus, Mars, Jupiter and Saturn, were easy to spot even without a telescope. Ancient Romans named them after their gods and goddesses, and many countries still use these names today.

### 15 JOHN MICHELL
*1724–1793, England*
Black holes are invisible places in space where the gravity is so strong, it pulls everything into it, *even light*, like a hole in quicksand. Michell predicted their existence way before anyone else. It was nearly 200 years before his theory was finally proven.

### 16 URANUS
*Discovered 1781*
The first planet to be discovered using a telescope. Most people thought it was a star, till astronomer William Herschel set them straight. Uranus was eventually named after the Greek god of the sky.

### 17 CECILIA PAYNE
*1900–1979, UK/USA*
No one knew what stars were made of. Then Payne discovered that they're burning balls of gas. (Mainly hydrogen and helium. Not the gas you get from eating too many sprouts.)

### 18 THE ISS
*21st century, 400 km above Earth*
The International Space Station. Astronauts from many countries stay up here for months at a time, performing experiments as it orbits Earth. You can spot it as it passes overhead.

### 19 SPUTNIK 1
*1957, Soviet Union*
This small satellite (about the size of a beach ball) was the first human-made object to orbit Earth. It beeped radio signals back to Earth for three weeks till its batteries died.

### 20 KATHERINE JOHNSON
*1918–2020, USA*
Getting astronauts to the Moon (and back) required a lot of clever maths. Johnson worked out how spacecraft could launch, travel and return safely to Earth. She didn't even need a computer.

### 21 WANG ZHENYI
*1768–1797, China*
People tried all sorts of ways to explain eclipses, from dragons eating the Sun to dogs trying to steal it. Zhenyi used a lamp, table and mirror to show that it's simply the Moon coming between Earth and the Sun.

### 22 APOLLO 11
*1969, USA*
Neil Armstrong, Buzz Aldrin and Michael Collins were the first astronauts to fly to the Moon, on the Apollo 11 mission. Poor Collins had to wait in the command module, while the other two got to bounce off giant craters.

### 23 FAR SIDE OF THE MOON
*First explored 2019*
One side of the Moon always faces away from us. Chinese probe Chang'e-4 was the first to land on this 'dark' side. Sadly, it confirmed that none of the Moon is made of green cheese.

### 24 HUBBLE SPACE TELESCOPE
*Launched 1990, USA*
This powerful telescope orbits high above Earth, and sends back astonishing information about the universe. An even more powerful telescope has just been launched, too.

### 25 SPACE JUNK
*20th/21st century, Earth's orbit*
Over 27,000 bits of space junk orbit Earth – mostly old satellites and leftover bits from space missions. Scientists have to keep track of it all, to avoid collisions.

# Do you see what I see?

## STARS AND CONSTELLATIONS ACROSS THE WORLD

Ever since ancient times, humans have looked up at the night sky and seen patterns in the stars.

These clusters of stars, called constellations, helped people navigate long before maps, compasses or GPS were invented. If you know the position of certain stars and constellations, and how they move across the night sky (and it isn't cloudy), you can work out which direction you're going in.

However, when different peoples looked at the stars above them, they joined the dots in many different ways, and saw amazingly different shapes. Here are some constellations that share at least one major star, but end up making very different figures.

Constellations featuring
**POLARIS (THE NORTH STAR)**

*Little Bear (Europe)*

*Twisted Foot (Central America: Aztecs)*

*Loon (North America: the Ojibwe people)*

*Woman's Chariot (Scandinavia: Norse)*

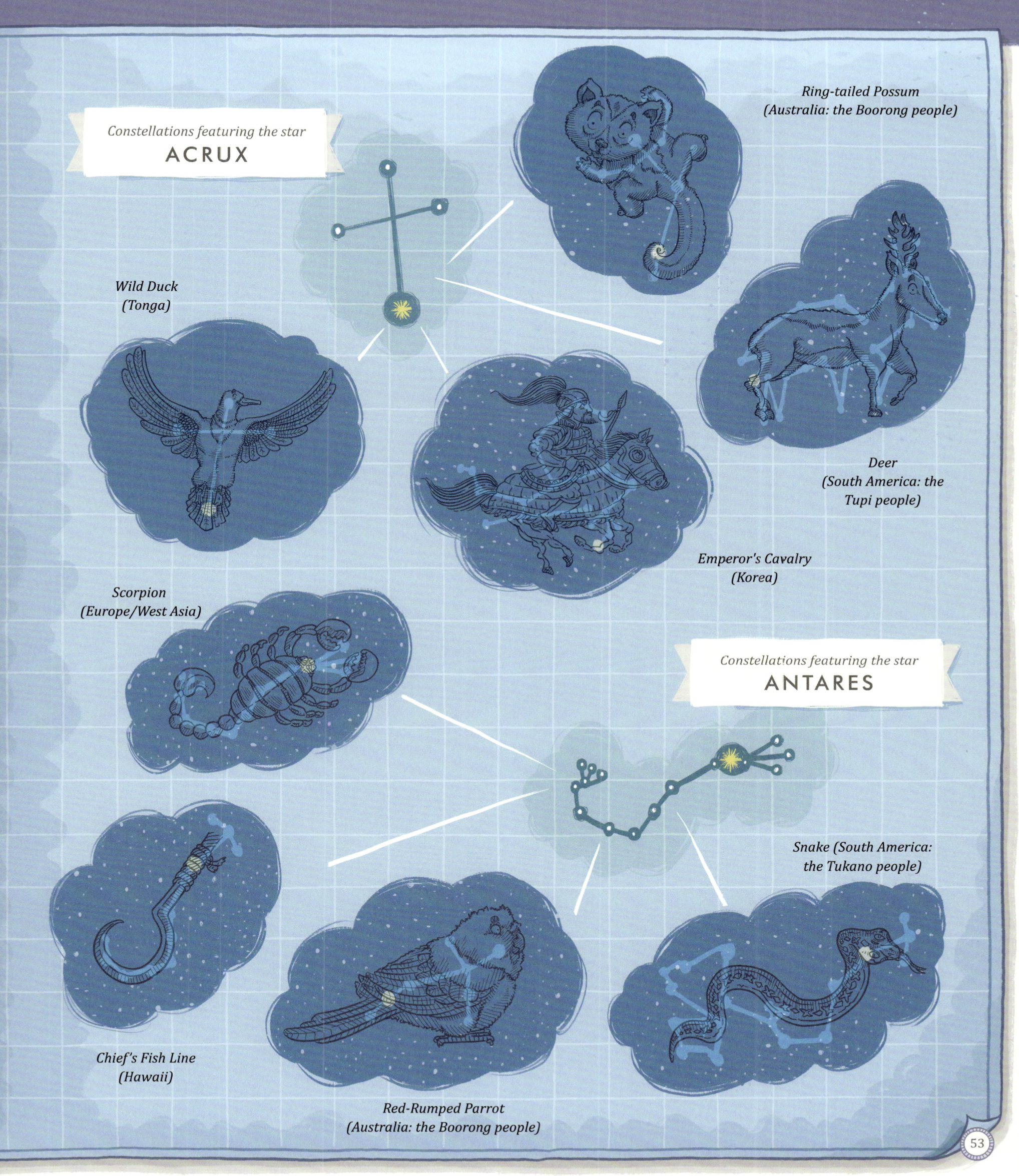

# Animals in space

## ALL ASTRONAUTS GREAT AND SMALL

Before they set off into space, people thought it might be a good idea to send some animals first – just to check that a living being could come back alive, and other little details like that. No one asked the poor creatures how they felt about this (sadly, animals rarely have a say in these matters.) But many did return safely, and scientists learned a lot from their experiences. These are just a few of the many animal astronauts.

### FRUIT FLIES

In 1947, fruit flies became the first critters to go into space. They were chosen because a lot of their genes are similar to ours. (This is probably as surprising to the flies as it is to us.)

### DOGS

In 1957, a stray dog called Laika became the first animal to orbit Earth. It was thought that a stray would cope better with the harsh conditions in space. She made it up into space, but sadly never came down.

### TORTOISES

In 1968, two Russian tortoises became the first animals to orbit the Moon and return to Earth. Unlike poor Laika they survived the trip, travelling at speeds that no other tortoise before or since has ever experienced.

### CHIMPANZEES

Chimps are our closest animal relatives, so scientists were keen to see how they'd fare in space. In 1961, a little chimp called Ham was blasted into space wearing a tiny spacesuit and a nappy. He'd been trained to pull levers, to show that it was possible to carry out tasks in space. Ham returned to Earth safely, and lived for many years.

## GOING TO THE LOO
Floating poo is a bad idea, so astronauts use tubes for weeing and special loos for the rest. And hold on tight so you don't float away.

## SLEEPING
You'll have to strap yourself to your sleep station, so you don't drift off (literally) in the middle of the night.

## EATING
Anything crumbly is off the menu, in case bits float into delicate machinery. So, goodbye toast . . .

## CLEANING YOUR TEETH
Astronauts mustn't spit toothpaste out or it will float around. The answer? Just swallow it.

## DRINKS
Even liquids float around, so forget about pouring juice into a cup. You'll have to drink from a pouch with a straw (but at least you won't have to wash up afterwards.)

# Living in space
### WHERE YOUR POO WON'T STAY IN THE LOO

Life on the International Space Station isn't easy, with everything floating about in free fall. If you want to be an astronaut, you'll have to learn how to do all sorts of everyday things in new and not very comfortable ways.
(Note: if these problems make you want to cry, the tears won't roll down your face. They'll just hover around your eyes in sad little spheres.)

# Tools of the Trade
## REACHING FOR THE STARS

### TELESCOPES

Look at the night sky, and you might be able to spot Saturn, some 1.5 billion kilometres away – but with a telescope you can see so much more. Four hundred years ago, the first telescope used two glass lenses to magnify the sky three times over. Today, enormous radio telescopes (some so big they occupy whole valleys) can spot stars millions of light years away.

### ROCKETS

American inventor Robert Goddard was convinced that one day we'd be able to send rockets to the Moon. In the early 1900s, he built all sorts of rockets, eventually managing to blast them nearly three kilometres into the sky. At the time people laughed at him. But decades later his theories helped get humans into space.

### SPACE PENS

Need to write in space? Easy, use a pen . . . or not. Sadly, without gravity the ink won't flow properly. And pencils can break and send bits of lead floating about. Luckily a man called Paul Fisher spent a lot of time and money creating a clever pen that could write upside down, and in boiling and freezing temperatures. It has been used on space missions ever since.

### MARS ROVERS

Humans haven't set foot on other planets yet, but we have built extraordinary vehicles which have landed on Mars. These rovers can be controlled from Earth and can take photos and videos, collect samples and perform complex experiments like analysing the soil and atmosphere. One even carried a helicopter. Not bad for a fancy, remote-controlled car.

# The discovery of
# Buildings

## MAKING LIFE COMFY, ONE BRICK AT A TIME

Nowadays most people live in buildings – you probably live in one yourself. But for hundreds of thousands of years, humans were on the move. We were hunter-gatherers, moving around with the seasons, searching for food. We might sleep in a handy cave, or knock up a simple shelter from rocks, wood or bones.

It was only when we worked out how to grow crops and keep farm animals that we started to settle down and build houses. First came small villages, then towns and cities. Along the way we invented all sorts of things that made life more pleasant, such as heating, plumbing, toilets and glass windows.

We started showing off, too, constructing enormous grand buildings, from pyramids to palaces and cathedrals. It takes vast numbers of people to build these structures, and they stand as amazing symbols of what we can achieve when we work together.

Today over half the world's people live in cities, and our buildings have a huge impact on the planet. Our aim now is to create homes that don't damage the environment (rather like our ancient human ancestors, tens of thousands of years before us.)

### FUNNY, THAT . . .
The *Sagrada Família* (it means 'Holy Family') is an astonishing church in Spain. The design of the building is so complicated, it's still not quite finished some 140 years after construction began in 1882. Builders tend to like a tea break, so they must have got through thousands of cuppas in that time.

# The discovery of Buildings

An architectural representation, depicting cosy caves, impressive pyramids and very pointy skyscrapers.

**1 EARLY DWELLINGS**
*From prehistoric times, worldwide*
Our hunter-gatherer ancestors created all sorts of amazing temporary homes. In the Ice Age, some built nifty huts using mammoth tusks and bones.

**2 GÖBEKLI TEPE**
*At least 11,000 years ago, Turkey*
This huge group of ancient temples was built by hunter-gatherers, before any towns or cities existed. Its massive stone pillars are covered with carvings of fierce creatures like vultures, spiders, snakes and scorpions.

**3 ANGKOR WAT**
*12th century, Cambodia*
Legend has it that this beautiful, massive city of elaborate temples was created by the god Indra in a single night. It was actually built by a huge bunch of people, and took over 30 years.

**4 TENOCHTITLÁN**
*14th century, Mexico*
The Aztecs built their capital city on an island in a lake. According to legend, the gods told them to settle on the spot where they saw an eagle perched on a cactus, eating a snake. Beats visiting lots of estate agents.

**5 BURJ KHALIFA**
*2010, Dubai*
The world's tallest building (currently). It's over five times taller than the Great Pyramid – but how long will it hold that record?

**6 THE FORBIDDEN CITY**
*1420, Beijing, China*
The imperial palace of the Chinese emperors. It was 'forbidden' because most people weren't allowed in, and only the emperor could walk about as he pleased. With over 900 beautiful buildings and gardens, it's a wonder he didn't get lost.

**7 LEANING TOWER OF PISA**
*Constructed 12th–14th century, Italy*
Pisa's bell tower is famous for being wonky. Built on soft ground, it started sinking halfway through construction. Amazingly, it's remained sort-of upright for over 600 years.

**8 CAVES**
*From prehistoric times, worldwide*
Most prehistoric people didn't live in caves. They just used them as safe spots to rest and shelter. Some cultures *did* live in caves, though, and still do: the town of Guadix in Spain has stylish houses carved into the hills.

**9 YURTS**
*From ancient times, Central Asia*
Brilliant, sturdy tents made from wooden frames, covered in felt. In the 1200s, Mongol emperor Genghis Khan conquered half the known world while lugging his yurt behind him.

**10 MEHRGARH**
*Around 9,000 years ago, Pakistan*
People lived in this Stone Age village an incredibly long time ago – but the small, square, mud-brick homes they built don't look that different from our modern houses.

**11 SHANGHAI TOWER**
*2015, China*
Big buildings use a lot of energy, but architects are trying to change that. This tower has over 200 wind turbines. They power its lights, saving energy (and the planet).

**12 CAHOKIA**
*11th–14th century, USA*
This Native North American city was one of the largest in the Americas. It had important buildings set on huge, hand-built earth mounds, and over 15,000 people lived here. Why they later abandoned it is a mystery.

**13 TAJ MAHAL**
*17th century, India*
A beautiful, white marble building, commissioned by emperor Shah Jahan as a tomb for his favourite wife, Mumtaz Mahal. We don't know how his other wives felt about this. Let's hope they didn't mind.

**14 POSTMAN CHEVAL'S PALACE**
*Built 1879–1912, France*
This astounding fairy-tale castle was constructed single-handedly by a postman called Ferdinand Cheval. Unsurprisingly, it took him 33 years to complete.

**15 THE GREAT PYRAMID**
*2560 BCE, Giza, ancient Egypt*
An immense tomb built for Pharaoh Khufu. It's made from over two million huge stone blocks, and was the tallest building in the world for nearly 4,000 years. Not bad for the house of a single dead guy.

**16 GREAT CITY OF BENIN**
*15th century, southern Nigeria*
The walls around Benin City were huge. In fact they were the largest structure in the world after the Great Wall of China. The city's streets were full of elegant houses. They even had an early form of street lighting.

**17 HANGING GARDENS OF BABYLON**
*Around 600 BCE, Mesopotamia*
The ancient city of Babylon is famous for its magnificent 'hanging gardens'. No one knows quite what they looked like, but they probably took one heck of a lot of watering.

**18 SYDNEY OPERA HOUSE**
*1973, Australia*
This astonishing concert hall was unbelievably difficult to build, but it was worth it. The finished opera house was so grand, it even had an opera written about it.

**19 ST BASIL'S CATHEDRAL**
*16th century, Moscow, Russia*
Tsar Ivan the Terrible (who really was terrible) had this extraordinary cathedral built to celebrate winning a battle. Many years later it was painted in crazy bright colours, long after old Ivan had kicked the bucket.

**20 COLOSSEUM**
*80 CE, ancient Rome*
This massive amphitheatre was the ultimate ancient sports stadium. It held wild-animal fights, gladiator battles – and lots of executions. It's even said that they flooded it, so they could stage mock sea battles.

**21 BIG BEN AND THE HOUSES OF PARLIAMENT**
*11th–19th century, London, UK*
The place where the British parliament meets was originally a royal palace. It was rebuilt after a huge fire destroyed most of it in 1834. Its clock tower contains Big Ben, a famous 13-tonne bell which bongs every hour.

**22 GREAT MOSQUE OF DJENNÉ**
*From 13th century, Mali*
This incredible temple is built almost entirely out of sun-baked mud bricks, covered in clay. It's been rebuilt three times and gets re-plastered with mud every year during a huge festival.

**23 CHRYSLER BUILDING**
*1930, USA*
In the early 1900s, New York architects were racing to see who could build the world's tallest building. The Chrysler Building took the biscuit, but kept its crown for barely a year, when it was beaten by the Empire State Building.

**24 EIFFEL TOWER**
*1889, France*
This gargantuan iron tower was constructed for the World's Fair in Paris. French critics hated it, and called it a piece of 'metal asparagus', but it's now one of the world's most popular tourist attractions.

# Creating Brasília

## A CITY WITH WINGS

Most big cities grow over time. Some parts may be planned with great care, but often buildings, roads and green spaces sprout up organically over hundreds or thousands of years, as people drift in and settle.

Brasília, the capital of Brazil (see what they did there?) is different. The whole city was built from scratch during four years between 1956 and 1960. The government's idea was to move the capital city away from the coast in Rio de Janeiro, and closer to the centre of the country. And they wanted this brand-new city to be super-modern. The original plan for Brasília is extraordinary. It looks like a giant insect or aeroplane, and it's full of amazing buildings. Now home to around three million people, it's still one of the most striking cities in the world, thanks to the efforts of three brilliant individuals:

**Roberto Burle Marx**
*designed the city's parks and gardens.*

Architect
**Lúcio Costa**
*designed the layout of the city.*

**Oscar Niemeyer**
*was the architect who created Brasília's boldly shaped and unusual buildings.*

NATIONAL CONGRESS | METROPOLITAN CATHEDRAL | PALACE OF JUSTICE | ITAMARATY PALACE

# Tools of the Trade
## HANDY HOME COMFORTS

### HEATING

For thousands of years, fire was the most popular way to keep your house warm. Fireplaces and ovens were used all over the world. But open fires can be dangerous and smoky, so our ancestors invented central heating. There's even an underfloor heating system in Korea that is over 3,000 years old.

### WINDOWS

Windows bring light and air into your house, but *glass* windows are quite a recent invention. Before them, people used all sorts of things to keep out the draughts: animal skins, mats, wood, horn, and even oyster shells. In medieval Europe, glassworkers turned windows into works of art, creating intricate mosaics of coloured glass and metal.

### LIGHTING

Humans aren't great at seeing in the dark, so we had to find ways to help us. Ingenious Stone Age peoples created candles inside scallop shells. They burned moss, soaked in the fat that dripped from their cooking fires. Burning things like candles, oil or gas was our main form of lighting until the nineteenth century, when light bulbs were invented.

### TOILETS

No one wants to live next to their own poo: it smells bad and can cause diseases. But how best to get rid of it? Early toilets were just big holes in the ground. Ancient Roman baths had communal toilet benches where 50 people could go at once. Thank goodness for today's individual loos!

# The discovery of the
# Invisible World

## NOW YOU DON'T SEE IT, STILL YOU DON'T

Humans have always been curious. Throughout history we've tried to understand how the world around us works. But there's a small problem: a lot of the key building blocks that make our world (and us) are invisible. Energy, light waves, sound waves, atoms, bacteria: for most of human history, we had no way of knowing such things even existed.

But as our ancestors looked around them, they couldn't stop asking questions. Why does fire burn? Why do objects fall when you drop them? What is air made of? What are *we* made of?

They developed theories about anything and everything, and had to imagine all the things they couldn't see.

Slowly we invented ways to observe and measure the world. With new tools and experiments we could reveal all sorts of invisible secrets. By testing our theories we could discover even more. Gradually we unearthed minute particles and huge galaxies.

Today we understand a lot about the invisible workings of reality. But each new discovery leads to a whole bunch of new questions. The more we know, the more there is to find out.

### FUNNY, THAT . . .
For centuries people believed that small critters like fleas, maggots and even mice appeared as if by magic from non-living things like rubbish, cheese or soil. They couldn't think how else maggots could turn up in rotting meat. It wasn't till the 1600s that some scientists started to suspect that they might actually reproduce like other animals.

# Let there be light
## ISAAC NEWTON AND THE THEORY OF LIGHT

It wasn't obvious from the start that Newton would become one of the greatest scientific geniuses of all time. It wasn't even obvious that he'd be a scientist – he actually started out studying law. But in 1665, while he was still at university, the Great Plague struck England. This terrible disease devastated London, killing up to a quarter of the population. Other parts of the country were affected, too, and Newton's college in Cambridge had to close.

Newton was stuck at home in the countryside for two years, with plenty of time on his hands. Being an industrious sort of chap, he decided to try and figure out how light works – as you do. What is it made of? What colour is it, and many other questions besides. Using prisms, mirrors and telescopes, he made many discoveries, and proved that what we see as white light actually contains all the colours of the rainbow.

Some of Newton's methods were unusual, like staring at the Sun for ages (something no one should ever do – it almost made Newton blind) and many people found him really annoying. He was also furious when his ideas weren't fully accepted straightaway.

Luckily, other scientists eventually er . . . saw the light, and understood the brilliance of his discoveries.

# Er, I think we just broke this...
## LISE MEITNER AND SPLITTING THE ATOM

Almost everything in the universe is made of atoms (including us). These little particles are so tiny, you could fit millions of them on the head of a pin. So who would have thought that you could split an atom apart, and release a huge amount of energy? Lise Meitner, that's who. This awesome Austrian scientist made one of the most important discoveries of the twentieth century.

It takes a lot of energy to hold an atom together. Meitner figured out that you can split an atom of uranium — something scientists had thought was impossible — and release some of that energy. It was a discovery that changed the world.

On the plus side, we can now generate electricity in nuclear power stations by splitting atoms. On the downside (and it's quite a big downside), Meitner's discovery was also used to create nuclear weapons — something she strongly disapproved of.

Did Meitner get the credit for her discovery? Not exactly. As a woman, she'd had to fight to be allowed to study science at all. And because she was Jewish, she had to flee to Sweden in 1938 to escape from the Nazis. So it was her colleague, Otto Hahn, who won the Nobel Prize for their work. Happily, Meitner went on to receive many other awards for her achievements. After her death, a chemical element, meitnerium, was named in her honour.

INVISIBLE WORLD

# Tools of the Trade
## THINKING BIG, SEEING SMALL

### ALEMBIC

This handy piece of kit has been around since ancient times. By heating things up on one side of it, then cooling them down on the other, you can separate one part of a liquid from another. Alembics were used to make medicines, perfumes and alcoholic drinks. Alchemists also used them to try and turn ordinary metal into gold. (Sadly, they failed.)

### PRISM

People originally used these pretty glass shapes for fun, holding them up to the light to see the colours of the rainbow inside. Then Isaac Newton realised he could use a prism to prove that white light was made of different colours. These days, prisms are used in everything from telescopes and microscopes to certain kinds of spectacles.

### MICROSCOPE

When microscopes were invented in the late 1500s, they completely changed the way we saw the world. Suddenly we could study minuscule objects and creatures that had literally been invisible to us. Some early microscopes could magnify objects 250 times, which seems a lot. Modern electron microscopes can enlarge things over a million times. Wow.

### LARGE HADRON COLLIDER

The parts of an atom are so small, we'll never be able to see them. However, scientists can smash them into one another in a particle accelerator, and study what happens when they collide. These racetracks for teeny-tiny things are surprisingly huge. Biggest of all is the Large Hadron Collider: a 27 km tunnel that loops under a mountain.

# The discovery of
# The Past

## WORKING OUT OUR PLACE IN HISTORY

We've always been fascinated by what came before us. How did we live in the past? What was the Earth like before humans came along? How did people cope before loos were invented? Many ancient cultures created fabulous myths and legends to explain how the world began. With modern knowledge and techniques, we can piece together a much more accurate picture of our planet's history.

However, it's not easy searching for the past. You have to dig up ancient, buried cities – or even more ancient fossilised dinosaurs. You have to decode languages no one speaks any more, and work out how people lived from small clues: shards of pottery, the remains of a hearth fire, or a few bones. It's like putting together a huge jigsaw puzzle, with most of the pieces missing. But with ingenuity and a lot of hard work archaeologists keep finding new and inventive ways to reach back in time.

The more we know about our past, the better we understand who we are now and how we got here. It's also a reminder that our here-and-now will be future people's distant past. What will those future people make of our lives and the clues we leave behind?

### FUNNY, THAT . . .
The tomb of Egyptian pharaoh Tutankhamun lay undisturbed for over 3,000 years. When it was discovered in 1922, a rumour spread that anyone who touched it would be cursed. Nonsense, surely? But then one of the people who'd entered the tomb suddenly died. Then the lights suddenly went out all over the city of Cairo. Spooky! (But still nonsense.)

# The discovery of The Past

An illuminating excavation, including old cousins, fluffy dinosaurs and tiny microbes.

**① AGE OF EARTH**
*Calculated 1956, USA*
How old is our planet? People made all sorts of guesses. Then scientist Clair Cameron Patterson worked it out by studying the chemistry of rocks. Earth is 4.55 billion years old (and still looking great.)

**② CYCLOPES**
*From 700 BCE, ancient Greece*
Ancient Greeks told lots of stories about these one-eyed giants. They may have got the idea from the fossilised skulls of huge, extinct elephant-like creatures. The skulls have a big trunk hole in the middle – a bit like a massive eye socket.

**③ FIRST LIFE ON EARTH**
*Discovered 20th/21st century, Australia*
We don't know how or when life on Earth began, but scientists have found traces of teeny bacteria in Australian rocks dating back 3.5 billion years – before our atmosphere even had oxygen. Breathtaking!

**④ DINOSAUR EXTINCTION**
*Discovered 1980, USA*
No one was sure why dinosaurs went extinct until Nobel Prize-winning scientist Luis Alvarez and his geologist son Walter figured out that a huge meteorite hit Earth around 66 million years ago, making things tough for the big fellas.

**⑤ JAMES HUTTON**
*1726–1797, Scotland*
The inventor of modern geology. Hutton noticed that the wind and sea wash away tiny particles of rock – which then very slowly settle to form new rocks. This told him that Earth must be much, much older than people thought.

**⑥ OLDEST HUMAN BURIAL**
*Discovered 20th century, Israel*
Humans have been looking after their dead for a long time, as this burial from around 100,000 years ago shows. Red-ochre stones were found nearby, which might have been used in a ritual.

**⑦ CUNEIFORM**
*Decoded 19th century, Europe*
This ancient way of writing goes back over 5,000 years. When it was decoded, scholars discovered laws, recipes and even the rules of a board game. There's still loads to translate. Fancy having a go?

**⑧ WILLIAM JONES**
*1746–1794, England*
Jones taught himself an astonishing 28 languages, including Latin, Greek and Sanskrit. He noticed similarities between them, and realised they must have all developed out of an earlier long-lost language.

**⑨ CHARLES DARWIN**
*1809–1882, UK*
Darwin developed a revolutionary theory: that all creatures on Earth, including humans, are related, and have all evolved from a long-ago ancestor. His theory completely changed how we understand the past.

**⑩ THE ROSETTA STONE**
*Discovered 1799, Egypt*
No one could read Egyptian hieroglyphs, until this stone was discovered. It has the same text carved in three languages, including hieroglyphs and ancient Greek. That meant brainy French scholar Jean-François Champollion could translate it.

**⑪ RICHARD III**
*Discovered 2012, UK*
Famously the last English king to die in battle, in 1485. For centuries no one knew where Richard was buried. Then archaeologists finally found him. Under a castle? A cathedral? A monument? No. Under a car park in Leicester.

# A very right Charlie
## HOW THE THEORY OF EVOLUTION CAME TO BE

Charles Darwin's dad had wanted him to study medicine, but Darwin was much more interested in plants and animals. When he was invited to go to South America in 1831, he leapt at the chance.

Darwin's journey on the H.M.S. *Beagle* turned into an extraordinary five-year voyage around the world. It took him to jungles and deserts, mountains and volcanoes. He saw giant tortoises and spiky iguanas. He discovered the huge fossilised bones of extinct animals (including the giant ground sloth below), and wondered why they'd all died out. He collected thousands of plants and animals, including hundreds that European scientists had never seen before.

### LONG-LOST GIANTS
Some amazing giant creatures used to walk the Earth, but they're sadly extinct today. For instance, here's Megatherium, an enormous ground sloth, up to six metres long. He and his mates spent their time peacefully chewing the cud, but disappeared after the end of the last ice age. Boooo!

### CASTOROIDES
Beavers the size of a bear, which waddled the Earth until about 10,000 years ago. We don't know if they built lodges like modern beavers. If they did, they'd be seriously big lodges.

One thing in particular puzzled him. At the Galápagos Islands on the equator he'd found lots of little birds that were similar . . . but different. Some had chunky beaks for eating seeds. Others had pointy beaks for sipping from cactus flowers. Could they all be descended from the same original species?

A radical idea started forming in Darwin's head. He realised that plant and animal species can change over time, as they adapt to the conditions where they live. What's more, all life on Earth is related. Every plant and animal is part of the same family tree, and everything evolved from an ancient, very-long-ago ancestor.

His theories went against all the beliefs of his time. But when Darwin finally published his book, *On the Origin of Species*, it became a bestseller — as did his later book about human evolution. Of course, some people didn't like being told they were related to apes. (No one knows what apes think about being related to *us*.) But over the years Darwin's ideas became more and more accepted, and have changed forever the way we view life on Earth.

## GLYPTODON

A giant armadillo, the size of a small car (that's very large for an armadillo.) It was covered in thick armour and whacked opponents with its massive chubby tail.

## ARGENTAVIS

Weighing 70 kilos and with a seven-metre wingspan, Argentavis was possibly the heaviest flying bird ever. It was so heavy, it may have had to glide off mountaintops, instead of lifting off from the ground.

THE PAST

# Cousins past removed

## HOMININS THAT CAME BEFORE US

Today, only one type of human lives on the planet: us. But it wasn't always like that. For a really, really long time, other kinds of human were around — our distant relatives. Scientists are still working out how closely we're all related. Meet some of the family.

**① AUSTRALOPITHECUS AFARENSIS**
*From 3.7 million years ago until 3 million years ago*
Shorter than us, with small heads (and brains), these guys could walk upright, as well as moving around in trees like apes. Their bodies were probably covered in hair, and they had strong teeth and jaws for eating fruit and leaves.

**② HOMO ERECTUS**
*From 2 million years ago until at least 250,000 years ago*
*Homo erectus* was around for a loooong time. Their bodies looked a lot like ours, but their brains were smaller. They made stone tools for cutting up meat, and we think they used fire for cooking.

**③ HOMO NEANDERTHALENSIS**
*From about 400,000 years ago until 40,000 years ago*
Neanderthals lived in Europe and Asia at the same time that we were evolving in Africa. They had big brains, and it seems they lived in a similar way to us. They even bred with our ancestors. Most of us today have some Neanderthal DNA.

**④ HOMO SAPIENS**
*From about 300,000 years ago*
That's us! We've only been around for a relatively short time, but we've made massive changes to the planet and the climate. Maybe we should go back to sitting on trees and eating berries . . .

# Ötzi the Iceman
## RE-CREATING ONE MAN'S PAST

When hikers found a body in the Alps in 1991, it was so well preserved in the ice, they assumed it must be someone who'd died quite recently. Then scientists examined the frozen corpse and found something extraordinary. The dead man, whom they called Ötzi, after the place where he was found, was over 5,300 years old. He was in amazingly good shape (despite bad teeth, sore knees, heart disease, gut parasites and a broken nose . . . )

Ötzi's body has since been tested, scanned and studied in all sorts of ways, giving scientists an incredible amount of information about him.

### HEIGHT AND AGE
About 1.6 metres tall, and around 45 years old (shown by analysis of his bones).

### FACE
Ötzi wasn't looking his best after 5,000 years, but facial reconstruction techniques show that he may have looked like this fella on the right. He had dark hair, and DNA analysis shows he had brown eyes.

### TATTOOS
Ötzi had over 60 tattoos, mostly small dashes around his worn-out joints and bones. Perhaps he believed tattoos had healing powers?

### FOOD
Undigested food in Ötzi's stomach shows that his last meal contained wheat, deer and ibex meat.

### CLOTHES
He'd been wearing leather shoes (but had lost one.) He also wore leather leggings, sheepskin and goatskin coats, and a bearskin hat. Fancy.

### HOW DID HE DIE?
This isn't very jolly. Poor Ötzi was stabbed, then a few days later an arrow in the shoulder finished him off. Stone Age life wasn't easy.

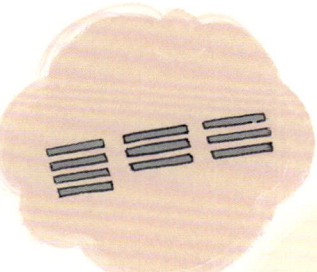

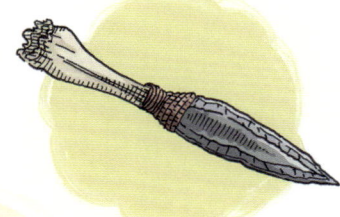

# Tools of the Trade
## DIGGING BACK IN TIME

### METAL DETECTOR

These nifty machines are handy for finding buried treasure. Wave one over the ground, and it'll bleep if there's metal below – great for archaeologists, as metal doesn't decay like wood or leather. Amateur detectorists have also made important discoveries, like the Staffordshire Hoard: a huge pile of gold and silver treasures, buried in England in the seventh century.

### CARBON DATING

How can we tell the age of a skeleton, or a piece of cloth? One useful clue is carbon-14. All living things on Earth contain carbon but after they die their carbon-14 starts to decay. By measuring how much carbon-14 is left, we can tell how long ago they lived. Carbon dating works on all organic things that are less than 50,000 years old.

### GIANT DRILL

If you want to know what the ground looked like millions of years ago, it's useful to have a giant drill. Archaeologists recently drilled down over a kilometre into the sea floor off the coast of Mexico. This allowed them to study cores of rock at the exact point where a meteorite hit Earth 66 million years ago, wiping out the dinosaurs.

### TROWEL, BRUSH, SPOON

Some of the most important tools for exploring the past are the simplest: shovels for digging a trench; trowels for gently scraping away dirt; brushes for cleaning delicate objects; sieves for sifting tiny things out of the soil. Even plastic spoons are handy for prising out ancient stuff without breaking it.

# The discovery of the Oceans

## TAKING THE PLUNGE

We live on a wet planet. In fact nearly three-quarters of Earth's surface is covered by water. We've been swimming, fishing, sailing and diving in it for thousands of years. (We've also been dropping tonnes of rubbish in it — we definitely need to stop doing that.)

Yet 80 per cent of the ocean is still a mystery to us, and we've mapped more of the surface of the Moon than we have of the ocean floor. But it's not an easy thing to do, even with modern, high-tech submarines. For a start, the ocean is unbelievably deep. If you dropped Mount Everest into the deepest ocean trench, that whole massive mountain would disappear below the surface. Imagine exploring over 10 kilometres down, in freezing pitch darkness, and with the crushing weight of all that water bearing down on you.

Until quite recently, we assumed that nothing could live in the deepest, darkest depths of the oceans, but we were wrong. We now know that all kinds of astonishing little critters live down there. As we've learned more about what goes on below the surface, we've discovered that a huge majority of the Earth's animals live in the sea — including some of the most unusual and surprising life forms on the planet.

### FUNNY, THAT . . .
Scientists were astounded to find that lobsters wee out of their faces, from nozzles under their eyes. If that doesn't sound bad enough, they also wee on *each other's* faces as a way to communicate. Still want to chat to a lobster? Maybe wear a mask . . .

10 TYRIAN PURPLE
*Around 3,500 years ago, Phoenicia*
This bright purple dye was incredibly rare and expensive. It was squeezed from yucky sea snails, and used to dye fancy clothes for kings and queens.

11 AMA DIVERS
*From 1st century?, Japan*
For some 2,000 years, these Japanese women have been diving into the ocean to harvest food and pearls. They can reach great depths, and carry on diving well into old age. Some are over 80 years old!

12 BULLWHIP KELP FARMING
*From ancient times, American Pacific Coast*
Native North Americans have long used this giant seaweed to make fishing ropes and nets. Kelp is also great at storing carbon, so restoring kelp forests around the world can help fight climate change.

13 DYKES
*Around 12th century, Netherlands*
Dykes are low walls that hold the sea back from the land. In the Netherlands, a lot of the country's land was reclaimed from the sea. Without dykes, it would be underwater.

14 ERNEST EVERETT JUST
*1883–1941, USA*
Some of the best ocean discoveries happen in a laboratory. By studying small sea creatures, Just made many important discoveries about how life begins from an egg.

15 OCEAN CURRENTS
*20th/21st century, USA*
In 1992, a container of bath toys accidentally fell in the ocean — and American scientist Curtis Ebbesmeyer saw an opportunity. By tracking where the toys washed up, he could see how ocean currents moved around the world.

16 THE GREAT PACIFIC GARBAGE PATCH
*From the 20th century, Pacific Ocean*
This is just rubbish. Literally. We throw millions of tonnes of plastic away every year, and a horrific amount of it ends up in the ocean. We should clean it up.

17 JACQUES COUSTEAU
*1910–1997, France*
This pioneering explorer helped develop the world's first scuba-diving equipment, as well as underwater cameras, and submarines for exploring the sea floor. (He also wore a tiny red hat.) His films, TV shows and books introduced millions to the wonders of the oceans.

18 THE BAJAU PEOPLE
*For centuries, southeast Asia*
The Bajau are nomads that live on the sea. They live on boats, or build houses on stilts over the water, and freedive deep underwater to catch their food.

19 TERRIBLE CREATURES
*From ancient times, worldwide*
Our ancestors thought the sea was full of scary monsters. It is, but maybe not the giants and sea serpents that they imagined. (And what they thought were mermaids turned out to be dugongs and manatees.)

20 JACQUES FRANCIS
*16th century, west Africa/England*
Most sixteenth-century Europeans couldn't swim, let alone dive, so skilled divers from Africa were in high demand. Francis had possibly trained as a pearl diver. He ended up leading the team that tried to salvage the *Mary Rose*, a valuable British warship.

21 COELACANTH
*Re-discovered 20th century, South Africa*
This huge, very ancient fish was thought to have gone extinct 66 million years ago, so the South African fishermen who caught a live one in 1938 were very surprised. Probably not as surprised as the poor coelacanth.

22 ROBERT BALLARD
*1942–, USA*
Ballard is a whizz at deep-sea exploration. He not only found the wreck of the *Titanic*, he also discovered hydrothermal vents — bizarre chimney-like structures that belch out boiling liquids from the sea floor.

23 GLOW-IN-THE-DARK SHARK
*Discovered 21st century, New Zealand*
What's better than a shark? A glow-in-the-dark shark! Scientists recently discovered that certain members of the bitey species can light up to blend with the ocean water and hide from predator and prey alike. Brilliant!

24 THE MARIANA TRENCH
*First explored 1960, Pacific Ocean*
The deepest place you can go in the ocean, 11 km below the surface. A submersible called *Trieste* was first to go down there in 1960. Fifty years later, filmmaker and explorer James Cameron reached it in his tiny one-man vessel.

# Sing a song of blubber
## THE MYSTERIES OF WHALE SONG

In the 1960s, American scientist Katy Payne made an incredible discovery. She was listening to a recording of humpback whale noises when she realised that it wasn't just a bunch of random sounds. It was a song!

Katy and her husband, fellow scientist Roger Payne, studied the whales' songs for many years. They discovered that only males sing – and they make the songs up together (a bit like a jazz band, but without the instruments.)

We don't know what the songs mean, but all the males in a particular group croon a version of the same song, which changes over the course of each year. The whales even borrow bits from other ditties they hear under the ocean.

Thanks to the whales' huge, resonating bodies, their songs can be heard several kilometres away. They can go on a while, too. Most songs last around half an hour, but the longest recorded was an epic 22 hours. Luckily the songs are strangely beautiful. In fact, when Roger Payne released an album of whale song, it became a surprise hit, selling over 100,000 copies.

Humpbacks themselves seem picky about what they listen to. When scientists in Hawaii played different songs to some local whales, the big fellas enjoyed their own recordings, but were sniffy about whale song from other parts of the world. Talk about liking the sound of your own voice.

# How low can you go?

## THE FISHY BUSINESS OF DEEP DIVING

Nowadays tiny submersibles can descend over 10 kilometres underwater, right down to the ocean floor. But it wasn't always like that. Here are some of the ways we've used over the centuries to dive down deeper – and stay down longer.

### DIVING BELLS

These crazy-looking contraptions worked by trapping air as they descended into the sea – like pushing an upturned cup into water. The idea goes back over 2,000 years. In fact, legend has it that Alexander the Great dived down inside a glass barrel. Rather more reliable diving bells are still used today.

### FREEDIVING

This is the daunting, dangerous activity of deep diving without any equipment at all. People have been doing it for millennia, and it takes a lot of skill and training. These days the best divers can dive down over 100 metres. Phew!

### EARLY DIVING SUITS

From the eighteenth century, people started making all manner of diving suits. Some were little more than fancy leather clothing, with a breathing tube up to the surface. Others were gigantic metal contraptions that made divers look like alien robots. But they (mostly) worked, and allowed divers to explore the ocean and salvage valuables from shipwrecks.

### COMPRESSED AIR

At last! The nineteenth century saw the invention of diving suits that really let divers breathe underwater, by carrying a tank of compressed air. Today's scuba gear is super-neat. Just add a mask, wetsuit and some rubber flippers and you're as close to a fish as you can get.

# Tools of the Trade
## HANDY WAYS TO EXPLORE THE DEPTHS

### SNORKELS

Snorkels make any trip to the seaside more fun. They're like giant straws that you can use to breathe when you're swimming underwater. The idea goes back thousands of years, long before plastic was invented. Divers in ancient Crete used hollowed-out reeds to breathe through, as they snorkelled around, harvesting sponges from the ocean floor.

### SONAR

This nifty technology was created to stop ships crashing into underwater rocks and icebergs, like the *Titanic* did. It sends a 'ping' sound through the water, and measures the time it takes to bounce back. If the ping bounces back quickly, it means an object is nearby. Dolphins use a similar technique to help them hunt. Pity we didn't ask them about it sooner.

### TEKTITE

In 1969, four ocean scientists bravely spent two months living 15 metres underwater in this pioneering research station. Living space was cramped and the food was awful, but it showed that humans could survive long periods of time underwater, and they could explore the ocean as never before. Over 50 'aquanauts' took turns to live down there.

### UNDERWATER ROBOTS

Even with today's high-tech diving suits and submarines, there are still places in the ocean where no humans can (or want to) go. Instead we've created robots to do the job for us. They can reach the deepest, darkest places, and can even explore the vast freezing seas beneath the Arctic ice sheets – all controlled by someone aboard a dry, cosy ship.

# The discovery of
# Ideas

## WHO WOULD HAVE THOUGHT?

Have we always lived the way we do today? Not really. Just think about some of the things we take for granted: that we divide our day into 24 hours; that it's a good idea to wear clothes; that all children should go to school. It's surprising to think that any of those things are new, but they're just some of the big ideas we've invented over the past several thousand years.

It's impossible to say exactly when a lot of these ideas started. Some of them happened so long ago, they've left no trace. You can't dig up an idea in the way you can dig up the ruin of an old building, or some ancient pots or bones.

That means a lot of the dates in this chapter are educated guesses. (At the moment: archaeologists and historians are finding new evidence all the time.)

Some ideas have proved popular all over the world, like taking the weekend off, paying for things with money, or having a national flag. Other things vary a lot from culture to culture.

Our ideas shape the world we live in. They've changed constantly over the last few thousand years, and will keep on changing as we (hopefully) try and find better ways to exist on our planet.

### FUNNY, THAT . . .
Some ideas never catch on because they're terrible. The inventors of *Smell-O-Vision* thought they'd enhance movie-goers' experience by filling cinemas with smells. In theory this would make the films seem more real. Sadly, audiences thought the idea stank.

**11 FOREIGN HOLIDAYS**
*From ancient times, Greece, Rome, Egypt*
We all love zooming off on holiday, and it's not a new thing. Ancient Greeks and Romans enjoyed a spot of tourism, too. They read guidebooks, travelled to admire famous cities and bought souvenirs.

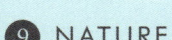

**10 SUSTAINABILITY**
*From ancient times, worldwide*
Even our ancient ancestors realised that it was a bad idea to cut down all the trees, or hunt animals to extinction. A hundred years ago, US scientist George Washington Carver showed how to grow crops without damaging the soil – and many pioneers like him are helping look after our planet today.

**9 NATURE**
*From ancient times, worldwide*
At some point in our history, lots of people began to think of themselves as somehow separate from nature, not part of it. Living in cities probably doesn't help. Perhaps if we accept that we're part of nature, we'll look after our planet better . . .

**8 NUMBERS**
*At least 5,000 years ago, Egypt/Mesopotamia*
Counting goes back over 30,000 years. Prehistoric people created 'tally sticks', by carving rows of lines on animal bones. Much later, ancient Egyptians and Mesopotamians both had the great idea of inventing symbols to represent numbers.

**1 GOVERNMENT**
*At least 5,000 years ago, Mesopotamia*
Over time, we've organised ourselves in lots of different ways. Perhaps small groups made decisions together, or single rulers ran things alone. Today's democratic governments only became common in the last couple of hundred years.

**2 EQUALITY**
*From ancient times, worldwide*
The idea that every person deserves to be treated equally is ancient, but people still have to work hard across the world today to make sure it's put into practice.

**3 SURNAMES**
*From ancient times, worldwide*
If you live in a small community, you only really need a first name. As our towns got bigger, it helped to have surnames, too. We often used our occupation, which is where names like Smith, Mason or Hunter come from.

**4 CLOTHES**
*About 170,000 years ago, Africa*
We've been wrapping up to keep warm for a very long time – and our Neanderthal cousins wore clothes, too. As societies developed, clothing became a way of showing your taste, wealth or particular place in society.

**5 HOMEWORK**
*19th century, Germany*
It seems German schoolchildren were the first to be clobbered with homework, and the idea soon spread around the world. Yay! Aren't you glad? No? Happily, some schools are now ditching the idea.

**7 TEENAGERS**
*1940s, USA*
For most of history, when you stopped being a child, you started being an adult. The idea that there might be a grumpy, rebellious stage in between began in America after World War II.

**6 FREE EDUCATION**
*18th century, worldwide*
It used to be a rare privilege to get a formal education (especially if you were a girl). Most people couldn't read or write. It was only a couple of hundred years ago that many countries started to realise that it was a good idea to educate everyone for free.

## ⑫ PETS
*From prehistoric times, worldwide*
The first animals we tamed were dogs. They were kept for practical reasons like hunting, but we think their owners cared about them, too. Pooches have been found buried alongside humans in ancient graves.

## ㉒ THE MIND
*From prehistoric times, worldwide*
Whether you call it the 'mind' or the 'soul', the idea that our thoughts and feelings are separate from our bodies is very ancient. Some philosophers say that, because each mind is unique, no one sees the same reality. Mind . . . blown.

## ⑬ MONEY
*From at least 5,000 years ago, worldwide*
For ages people just used to swap things: a fish for a loaf, or a horse for a fence. Then some bright spark thought of using tokens instead. Shells, whale teeth and even rocks were used before metal coins were finally invented.

### The discovery of
# Ideas
A blaze of blue-sky thinking, depicting prehistoric pets, lazy weekends and, er . . . homework.

## ㉑ COUNTRIES
We've had villages and city-states for thousands of years, but it took a long time to divide the world into countries. Ancient Egypt was one of the first, some 5,100 years ago (although its boundaries are different today.) Many countries only got their names and shapes in the last couple of hundred years.

## ⑳ OFFICES
*16th century, Florence, Italy*
Millions of people today work in offices, but they're quite a new idea. Previously most people worked in or around their home. The Uffizi in Florence is a famous art gallery now, but it was one of the first purpose-built office buildings. Its name means . . . 'Offices'.

## ⑭ PROPERTY
*Around 12,000 years ago, worldwide*
When did we start fencing off bits of land and claiming them as our own? It may have been when we started farming the land, instead of hunting and gathering.

## ⑲ LAWS
*Over 4,000 years ago, Mesopotamia*
We all need rules. The earliest surviving set of laws is the Code of Ur-Nammu, created by those clever Mesopotamians. Laws today vary a lot around the world. Things that are crimes in some countries are fine in others.

## ⑮ HOURS
*Around 3,500 years ago, ancient Egypt*
Ancient Egyptians were the first to split day and night into 24 chunks, but their hours were longer or shorter according to the seasons. The idea of 24 equal hours didn't catch on till accurate mechanical clocks became popular in the 1300s.

## ⑱ WEEKENDS
*20th century, USA*
Most people used to have just one day off a week, often for religious reasons. Over the past century, most countries finally started giving workers two days off. Now some countries are trialling a three-day weekend. Sounds great!

## ⑰ PUBLIC SERVICES
*From ancient times, worldwide*
What services should a country provide for you? Clean drinking water? A safe system for getting rid of everyone's poo? Free health care? All these ideas go back to ancient civilisations (though many people still don't have them today.)

## ⑯ CITIES
*Around 6,500 years ago, Mesopotamia*
From small villages and towns, we eventually created large cities. One of the earliest we know of is Uruk, which grew to house over 60,000 people. It had beautiful buildings, tall walls – but not a lot of loos.

# Great philosophers
## WISE GUYS WHOSE IDEAS SHAPED OUR WORLD

Philosophers think for a living. They ponder big questions like, 'What's the meaning of life?' and, 'Is broccoli better than bacon?' Here are six famous philosophers whose ideas had a huge impact.

### CONFUCIUS
(also called Zhongni)
*551–479 BCE, China*

Confucius taught that you shouldn't do anything to other people that you wouldn't want them to do to you. Good idea.

### SOCRATES
*Around 469–399 BCE, ancient Greece*

Socrates believed we should strive to live a good, moral life. He developed his ideas by asking tricky questions like, 'What makes us happy?' and, 'What is love?'

### AVICENNA
(Also called Ibn Sina)
*980–1037, Uzbekistan/Iran*

Avicenna was a thinker, doctor and scientist who taught that, if you wanted to find the truth about reality, you had to test your ideas using logic.

### RENÉ DESCARTES
*1596–1650, France*

Descartes questioned everything – even whether or not he existed. He decided that he *did* exist (phew!) because he was able to think – hence his famous saying: 'I think, therefore I am.'

### W.E.B. DU BOIS
*1868–1963, USA*

Du Bois was a philosopher, writer and activist who studied racism in America. He explained how seriously it affected Black people's lives, and argued passionately for justice and equality.

### SIMONE DE BEAUVOIR
*1908–1986, France*

De Beauvoir argued that men and women should be equal, and that women should have as much freedom as men to choose the kind of life they want to lead.

# You're absolutely rights

## THE UNIVERSAL DECLARATION OF HUMAN RIGHTS

It seems a pretty basic idea that governments should treat you well no matter who you are, but throughout history many societies have failed to do so.

After the horrors of World War II, the United Nations decided to create a list of rights that every person should have. Representatives from all around the world met to agree what these ideals should be. Together they wrote a declaration setting out 30 basic rights and freedoms — you can see a few of them listed on this scroll.

Happily, almost every country signed up to the Declaration. Unhappily, not everyone respects it, and many people around the world still don't enjoy these basic rights. While this still happens, it's our job to look out for our fellow humans and make sure they are all loved and respected equally.

Here are some of the key rights and freedoms in the Declaration.

Everyone has the right to:
- Life and freedom
- Equal treatment
- Freedom from slavery
- Freedom of opinion and expression
- Freedom of religion
- Equality in law
- Work
- Education
- Food and health care
- Privacy
- Peaceful protest

# We can all say that

## INVENTING A COMPLETELY NEW LANGUAGE

Here's an idea: what if everyone in the world could speak the same language? If we could all understand each other, would it make the world a more peaceful place? That was the dream of Polish doctor Ludwik L. Zamenhof. He dedicated his life to creating a whole new language, and he wanted it to be so simple anyone could learn it.

In 1887 he published a book to teach people his new language, which was nicknamed 'Esperanto' (meaning 'he who hopes'). At first there was a lot of interest in it, but not many people use it today. Fancy learning? Here are a few words to start.

| ENGLISH | ESPERANTO |
|---|---|
| HELLO | SALUTON |
| GOODBYE | ADIAŬ |
| DAY | TAGO |
| NIGHT | NOKTO |
| FATHER | PATRO |
| MOTHER | PATRINO |
| BOY | KNABO |
| GIRL | KNABINO |
| HOUSE | DOMO |
| DOG | HUNDO |
| CAT | KATO |
| LUNCH | TAGMANĜO |
| DINNER | VESPERMANĜO |

# Tools of the Trade
## HELPING IDEAS GET AROUND

### RHETORIC

Rhetoric is the ancient art of public speaking. It's an important skill to master if you want to convince other people to do things. For ancient Greeks and Romans, learning how to win an argument was a key part of a posh education. Students learned all sorts of tricks, such as speaking clearly and convincingly, and stirring up the audience's emotions.

### COFFEE-HOUSES

How can a hot drink spread ideas? When drinking coffee became popular, people quickly realised that it was nice to sip it in a café while having a really good chat. From the 1500s, coffee-houses popped up everywhere from western Asia to Europe. They became great places for philosophers, scientists, travellers and politicians to meet and discuss all sorts of new ideas.

### PAMPHLETS

These little booklets were a bit like mini newspapers or leaflets. They were cheap, quick to print – and easy to hide. That made them perfect for spreading radical new ideas. They were especially popular in Europe in the 1500s and 1600s, and helped spread all sorts of political and religious ideas. (And lots of nasty gossip and rumours, too.)

### THE INTERNET

The internet has shaken up our world even more than the printing press did 500 years ago. We can now share our best ideas (and our daftest ideas) all around the world in an instant. We're still learning how to deal with so much knowledge (and trying to work out what's fake and what's real), but our ideas and societies have benefited immensely from it.